SHAPE Your *life*

A 5-Step Blueprint
for Sustainable Stress Management

WENDY GARVIN MAYO, APRN, ANP-BC

Table of Contents

Step 4: Plan

Step 5: Execution

Foreword

The hesitancy of human beings to fulfill their potential arises not from the doubt of their abilities but their belief in what others have told them about themselves. Many of us daily await the approval of others to define our successes and failures. But if we simply just be, wait patiently, and have an unwavering belief that we can succeed despite our circumstances and not doubt, our destiny can be fulfilled.

Do not condemn yourself. You are not perfect. No one is, and that is okay. The stress of not accepting the normalcy of imperfection and the focus on one's faults causes the human body to turn against itself. When the body turns against itself in a state of stress, physical illness, mental illness, and spiritual distress can occur.

Wendy Garvin Mayo is a healthcare practitioner, stress solution strategist, emotional intelligence consultant, advocate, and life coach who has made it her life's mission to help others realize their potential. In realizing one's potential, stress and coping are factors that cannot be ignored.

Although positive, the associated hard work, dedication, and time commitments to achieve one's dreams and goals require work-life balance. In this book, Wendy Garvin Mayo provides readers with the tools to identify signs and symptoms of stress in their lives, the causes of stress, and if the stress is working to positively shape their potential or is destroying their physical, mental, and spiritual health.

This book is a great read throughout the lifespan of dreamers and goal-setters alike and for those who want to learn to prioritize and maintain their health.

Cheryl Green,
PhD, DNP, RN, LCSW, CNL, CNE, MAC, FAPA
Off-Shift Nurse Administrative Manager, Bridgeport
Hospital Milford Campus Yale New Haven Health
Doctor of Nursing Practice Chair and Committee
Member, Abilene Christian University

Introduction

In August 2000, on a hot, sunny day, I found myself in the car with my mom, Jean; sister, Luanne; and aunt, Merle. I had just left my home in the inner city of Boston, armed with my trusted navy blue Boston Red Sox t-shirt. We were headed to a place that seemed a world away, to the suburbs of West Hartford, Connecticut, where I was about to start my college experience. I felt increasingly excited as the car turned into the long tree-lined driveway of Saint Joseph College, drove past the huge quad covered with fresh green grass, and entered into a cloud of smoke from a nearby barbecue grill. As the smoke cleared, I saw fresh-faced students and apprehensive parents unpacking their trunks and suitcases from their vehicles.

Soon, it was my turn. We joined the crowd in unloading our car and hauling my stuff up to the third floor of Madonna Hall. After we finally got my keys from my Resident Assistant, unpacked, and decorated my new room, we proceeded outside and plopped under a large tree for some rest and recovery. As we relaxed in the shade, we were soon approached by an upperclassman.

"Hi, I'm Melissa," she greeted me. "What's your name?"

"I'm Wendy, from Boston," I answered as I waved my hand.

"What's your major?" Melissa inquired.

"Nursing!" I replied with a feeling of pride and a confident smile on my face.

Melissa looked at me with a raised eyebrow and pursed lips. "That's a tough major, and many of us don't make it out of the program," she commented as she pointed to her brown-skinned hand, giving me my first indication that Black and Brown people tended to have a different experience at this school. "I think there are only two of us in the program."

My smile faded, turning into a frog in my throat. My heart was pounding hard enough that I could hear it loud in my ears. The instant fear I felt soon turned to negative self-talk. I wondered, *Should I go with my backup plan of becoming a teacher? Should I have just gone to community college?*

I tried to hide this newfound stress behind a strained smile as Melissa walked away, but apparently, I didn't fool my mother. She looked at me, scoffed, and insisted, "You can do any damn thing you put your mind to." Her words gave me some comfort, but I wasn't totally convinced.

Despite my increasing feelings of doubt, I moved forward as a nursing student. I quickly found that I needed to weather a lot of stress in order to excel in the program. As a freshman, I encountered an overwhelming amount of information that needed to be mastered, from prerequisites for anatomy and physiology to pharmacology and pathophysiology–it seemed like there was a never-ending list of topics that had to be understood immediately.

In addition to the academic demands, I also had to quickly develop clinical skills critical for patient care, such as taking vital signs and the five rights of administering medication, which all had to be executed with precision and accuracy. The pressure to perform well and deal with the high-stakes nature of the profession was intense.

Through all of this, I had to figure out how to maintain some semblance of a work-life balance without getting overwhelmed by long hours of studying, attending lectures and clinics, and completing assignments. I also struggled with feeling like I had to compete with my fellow students. I was constantly waging a battle against exhaustion and burnout while keeping up my grades.

Being a Black girl at a predominantly white college also came with its own unique challenges and opportunities. While it gave me the chance to share my culture with others, educate my friends about my unique experiences, and help me develop resilience, strength, and self-confidence, it was also difficult at times. Because few people at my school shared my cultural experiences, I sometimes felt lonely or isolated from the campus community. I also occasionally felt marginalized and underrepresented on campus. Schools like mine often lacked diversity among faculty and staff, which made it harder to seek academic and emotional support from my professors and the administration.

These factors added to one central theme: undergraduate nursing school was stressful. I tried to hold these feelings in, keeping my doubts to myself and not letting my worries show in my words and actions. While my peers and professors may have thought I was handling things just fine, my mind kept returning to my initial encounter with Melissa. What if I was one of those people who didn't make it? Eventually, I learned to let this source of stress give me fuel. *I have to get this done*, I would often think to myself. *I have to make it through to the end.*

Ultimately, I did succeed. I finished my program and went on to a successful career in caring for people with cancer. The stress certainly didn't go away with graduation—nursing can certainly be a stressful career—but I got increasingly better at responding to stress in healthy ways and letting feelings of pressure drive me forward.

"I am so stressed." How many times have you said these words? How many times have other people taken you seriously when you said it?

Feeling stressed is such a common complaint that it's hardly even noteworthy. It's simply the norm. This is especially true when you're living in a world where everything is fast-paced, and there is just *so much* to do every day. You've got to get yourself looking presentable, embark on your commute, manage problems at work, sit in rush hour traffic again, drive the kids to their activities, prepare food, do the dishes, put in a load of laundry, clean up around the house, and then get ready to do it all again tomorrow. Chances are, your list is longer than the number of hours you have in a day, even when you don't include the activities you wish you had more time for, such as spending quality time with your partner or children, checking in on family members, or socializing with friends. You may even be so used to this routine that you equate feeling stressed with being productive. It's no wonder so many of us constantly feel like we're drowning.

Much of our stress is the result of habits that have a negative impact on our lives. You may let little things slide here and there, and before you know it, these behaviors become your standard operating procedure. You decide just this once to settle for less than what you want, and it becomes easier to settle again next time, even though it makes you unhappy. We create our own stress and become less capable of dealing with it effectively.

To make matters worse, most of us don't know how to properly deal with stress. This phenomenon is a normal part of life, yet very few people know where to learn tried-

and-true stress management methods. Many of us are just doing the best we can to keep our heads above water while not having the resources to navigate toward calmer water.

The great news is that it doesn't have to be this way. Stress management involves skills that you can learn, practice, and improve. With new tools, you can achieve a happier, healthier, more peaceful life more effectively.

How do I know that such a calm existence is possible? Because I have lived it, and I have helped others live it, too. My life path has carried me from oncology nursing to other roles in the healthcare industry to creating an entire career helping others learn about stress management and emotional intelligence.

As a part of this mission, I have founded two companies: SHAPE Partners, which empowers cancer patients' caregivers and loved ones to reduce stress and improve their mental health, and The Stress Blueprint, which teaches and empowers individuals and teams to manage stress by leveraging emotional intelligence so they can regain control of their lives and live a purposeful life. We use evidence-based stress management and psychology practices to help people who want to boost their quality of life. I also host the Nurse Wellness Podcast and run a Stress Blueprint Academy mentorship program to assist overwhelmed and burned-out nurses and healthcare professionals in navigating the rewarding but stressful field of healthcare. I have created, refined, and implemented many stress management techniques to help countless individuals explore their own passions, purpose, and pathway to take concrete steps toward their goals while aligning with their purpose.

Nearly all of the people who have participated in my stress management training and programs have successfully reduced their stress levels, often by significant amounts. People who use the tools that I have developed say that they feel empowered to manage their personal and workplace stressors, align with their purpose, and understand themselves and their stressors better are able to set and meet big goals and take better care of themselves.

My passion lies in empowering individuals to control their stress so they can be their best, do their best, and give their best in the world. And yes, this includes YOU!

This book will show you exactly how to move from where you are now to where you want to be.

Together, we will break down and explore all of the different strategies that you will use to reach your goals. Along the way, I will share my personal journey toward conquering stress, provide opportunities for reflection, and suggest activities to help you immediately dive in and find your own path toward a more peaceful existence. This book will help you discover how to:

- Understand where you are now and identify what led you down this path
- Pinpoint the goals and vision you have for your future

- Determine what you still need to fulfill your goals and find the necessary resources
- Create an action plan
- Carry out and stick with your plan with the help of a supportive network

This process will start with getting better acquainted with that pesky little problem called stress.

We will learn more about what it is and its effects on your mind and body. I will then introduce you to my proven method for fighting through ongoing cycles of stress to get to the place you want to be and live your best life. I call this process the SHAPE Framework.

What Stress Looks Like

"It is not stress that kills us,
it is our reaction to it."

—Hans Selye

It was the mid-1920s. A precocious eighteen-year-old Austrian-Hungarian man named Hans Selye was in his second year of medical school at the German University of Prague in the Czech Republic. As part of his training, he was required to go on rounds with his fellow medical students, observing and learning from the patients in the hospital. The patients all suffered from different types of serious injuries or chronic illnesses—burns, cancer, tuberculosis, and more. As a result of their conditions, the patients experienced a wide range of symptoms. However, the things they had in common struck the young Dr. Selye as noteworthy.

All of the patients seemed to share a few key symptoms. They were extremely tired, wanting to lie down most of the day. They didn't eat much, causing the pounds to drop off. Most of them were in low spirits; they didn't really take much interest in going to work or doing any of the activities they usually liked to do. They just looked sick. This common set of symptoms conflicted with the current medical curriculum, Dr. Selye noticed.

In the early 20th century, doctors generally believed that each form of illness came with specific symptoms that could be used to diagnose the condition and track the disease's progress over time. Medical experts practicing in this era didn't realize that chronic conditions could cause similar complaints. Dr. Selye was the first to pinpoint what he called "general adaptation syndrome" or, more simply, the "syndrome of just being sick."

While Dr. Selye found his observations curious, he didn't immediately do anything with the information. He graduated from medical school. He got a Ph.D. in organic chemistry. He completed a research fellowship at McGill University in Montreal, Canada, studying hormones.

It was at McGill that he again noticed a general set of symptoms that accompanied sickness, but this time, the symptoms occurred in laboratory rats. When the rats were injured, given certain drugs, forced to be extremely physically active, or exposed to cold temperatures, they also seemed to look sick. Finally, about a decade after his initial observations in hospital patients, he published a paper outlining his basic theory. What was the culprit that connected all of these individuals? Dr. Selye blamed stress.

Today, Hans Selye is known as the father of stress research. He was the first to introduce the world to stress theory—the idea that certain factors can put pressure on the body, leading to ongoing biological changes and decreased health. While other researchers had previously discovered that our bodies can change when we suddenly find ourselves in a dangerous situation, Dr. Selye was the one to describe the ongoing, long-term effects of putting ourselves in uncomfortable situations. After his initial publication, Dr. Selye went on to conduct much more research studying the processes in our bodies that underlie the stress response. His work serves as the foundation of everything we know about stress today.

What Is the Purpose of Stress?

Why do we even have to experience stress? It turns out that stress is a type of survival mechanism that evolved to help keep us safe. Stress responses helped our ancestors survive dangerous situations and live longer lives. Today, our bodies use stress to react to many different types of demands or threats. When you detect danger—whether real or imagined, whether a physical risk or a mental challenge—your body's defenses automatically ramp up in a process known as the "fight-or-flight" reaction or the "stress response."

Dr. Selye defined stress as "the non-specific response of the body to any demand for change." He proposed that when some type of stressor was present—when some external factor required you to mentally or physically change—your body would first respond by going into crisis mode. Biological processes such as the fight-or-flight response would then be activated in an attempt to resist the stressor and keep things running smoothly. Finally, the body would become exhausted, leading to the familiar symptoms of sickness and fatigue. In this way, Dr. Selye believed our bodies would try to adapt to new situations but eventually use up all of our energy. In the end, ongoing stress becomes too much for us to deal with.

In recent years, other experts have built on this initial model of stress. Stress has also been defined as the physical, mental, or emotional strain or tension that occurs when you believe that the demands being placed on you eclipse the personal and social resources you can effectively use.

In other words, stress in your body is like a rubber band being stretched to its limits. As the rubber band—or your body or mind—is stretched, it's constantly trying to resist the change.

Eventually, however, the rubber band may snap or may remain stretched out, just as your body and mind undergo permanent changes in response to never-ending stress.

How stress affects you depends, at least in part, on how you perceive it. While some of us dread performing or speaking in front of an audience, others thrive in the spotlight. Where one person may operate best under pressure and with a short deadline, another will become paralyzed with fear as job demands increase. While you might like providing care for your parents, your siblings might find the duties to be too much to handle. What's stressful for you may not be for someone else and vice versa.

Can We Control Our Stress?

We are all affected by stressors. As Dr. Selye put it, "Stress is part of life." Stressors are typically thought of as being harmful, such as working a demanding job schedule or living in a tumultuous relationship. But anything that asks a lot of you might be stressful. This includes happy occasions like planning a wedding, purchasing a home, enrolling in college, or being promoted.

In our modern world, stressors come in both external and internal forms. **External stressors** are things in your environment that you don't have much control over. They may be physical factors, such as piles of clutter sitting in your house or a loud work environment.

External stressors also include events. They may be minor events, such as dealing with an inconsiderate individual or getting ready for a big deadline at work, or major events, like getting fired or dealing with the loss of a loved one. Major worldwide events such as the COVID-19 pandemic also certainly qualify as external stressors. While we don't often have much power over these external stressors, we still have some control over our reactions to them.

Of course, not all stress is brought on by outside forces. **Internal stressors** come from within us. They include our thoughts, beliefs, and life choices. Internal or self-generated stressors may include negative self-talk, having low self-esteem, looking at things through a pessimistic lens, setting standards for yourself that aren't realistic, or worrying about something that might or might not happen. Although it can be challenging, you have full control over your relationship with these internal stressors.

Both external and internal stressors can lessen when you adopt a growth mindset. This type of outlook can allow you to set healthier intentions for yourself, gain clarity on your life purpose, engage in wellness practices that optimize your health, and ultimately put you in a place to transform your life.

Some Types of Stress Are Worse Than Others

Your body uses its stress reaction as a form of defense. When functioning properly, it aids in maintaining your energy, focus, and alertness. Stress can be life-saving in emergencies, providing you the extra stamina to defend yourself or causing you to slam on the brakes to prevent a collision, for example.

Stress can also sharpen your instincts and keep you on your toes. Think back to the last time you faced a major challenge at work or school. You may not have felt good at the moment, but that extra pressure may have helped you think more clearly and perform at a higher level.

Hans Selye even developed a rhyme to describe this phenomenon:

"Fight always for the highest attainable aim But never put up resistance in vain."

Dr. Selye felt that a little bit of resistance—in other words, stress—was sometimes worth it to achieve the things you are aiming for. Stress may help keep you sharp during a presentation at work, focus more clearly when you're trying for a game-winning free throw, or motivate you to study for a test you're worried about even though you'd rather watch TV. Stress can push you past obstacles that otherwise might hold you back.

When stress is positive or feels good, it is called **eustress**. This "happy stress" also occurs during major positive life events, such as receiving a surprise marriage proposal or finding out you are having a baby (as long as you are planning to have one). It can boost your mood, make you feel excited, boost your well-being, and help you feel more content. In other words, it has the opposite effects as some of the more negative forms of stress.

Although not all stress is harmful, beyond a certain point, it ceases being beneficial and begins to do serious harm. Overwhelming stress can have a detrimental effect on your health, mood, productivity, relationships, and quality of life.

Short-term stress, also called acute stress, is caused by an immediate catalyst and disappears quickly. Picture laying in bed at night watching television, and suddenly the electricity goes out, followed by booming thunder and lightning brightening up your room. Moments later, the electricity returns, and the thunder and lightning subside like a tidal wave crashing on the shore. Just as the storm quickly recedes and your house adapts to the sudden loss of power, short-term stress forces your body to quickly readjust and then gradually recover.

Episodic stress lasts slightly longer than short-term stress. We experience episodic stress when short-term stress happens over a period of time. This may occur when you have too much on your plate. Just as you conquer one stressful task, another rears its head. You may get little breaks here and there, but another stressor is always just around the corner.

The worst type of stress is **chronic stress.** This is a prolonged form of stress that occurs when you find yourself in long-term situations that are unpleasant or painful. You may experience chronic stress if you are living with an ongoing illness, find yourself stuck in an unhappy relationship or at a difficult job, are constantly struggling with your finances, or are serving in a caregiving role for a loved one. We all also experienced chronic stress as the world changed around us during the COVID-19 pandemic.

Chronic stress is serious. It can have significant impacts on our health and may even be dangerous in the long term. This is the type of stress we need to work hardest to avoid.

However, getting ourselves out of situations that cause chronic stress may require taking big steps and making significant life changes. That's exactly what this book will empower you to do.

How Stress
Changes Our Bodies

"I promise you nothing is as chaotic as it seems.
Nothing is worth diminishing your health. Nothing is
worth poisoning yourself into stress, anxiety, and fear."

—Steve Maraboli

In his research, Dr. Selye witnessed such a strong connection between stress and health that he believed that many of the most common illnesses were a direct result of stress. While later research has found that not quite to be the case—we now know of many other factors that can also lead to disease—it is certainly true that stress can cause or worsen some health conditions and greatly impact mental and physical health.

The Stress Response in Two Phases

The stress response contains two phases that help us deal with different types of threats. The first phase is a short-term reaction controlled by the sympathetic adrenal-medullary (SAM) system. This reaction helps you make better decisions about a threat by making you more alert and more capable of assessing and responding to risks. It's like a smoke detector that sends out an initial alarm when there's a fire to alert the members of the house—or, in this case, the other organs and tissues in your body—that there's nearby danger.

It all starts with your hypothalamus, the "command center" in your brain that helps control your hormones and nervous system. When the hypothalamus detects a stressful situation, it sends out signals telling the medulla (inner part of the adrenal glands) to produce stress hormones like adrenaline and noradrenaline. These hormones cause a cascade of symptoms in the face of a possible threat:

- Your heart beats faster so that more blood can be delivered around your body, and you are prepared for action.

- Your blood pressure rises.

- You breathe faster and deeper, and your lungs take in more oxygen.

- Your pupils dilate.

- Your senses (sight, sound, smell, taste, and touch) become more keen.

- More sugar enters your bloodstream, and your metabolism is boosted, giving your cells a larger supply of fuel and increasing your energy.

- Your body slows down organs and tissues that it doesn't immediately need, including your digestive system, immune system, and tissues that make hormones.

- Blood and oxygen rush to your brain, muscles, and other essential organs that you may need for fighting or running away.

- You become more alert and less sleepy.

- These changes prepare your body for swift action. They are intended to get you out of danger as quickly as possible. It's similar to how you might take action when faced with a fire: if you hear the smoke detector go off, you may grab a fire extinguisher or call 911 to ask for a fire truck.

This type of stress response is short-lived; your body can't keep it up forever. Once short-term stress passes, levels of stress hormones will drop, and your body processes will go back to functioning as they normally do. Or at least, that's how your body ideally works. If you're faced with episodic or chronic stress, these systems will remain activated, continuously flooding your body with hormones.

If you're faced with a threat that is more serious or lasts for more than a few minutes or so, your hypothalamus will release another substance called corticotropin-releasing hormone (CRH). This hormone activates the pituitary gland, which sets off a different type of stress response called the hypothalamic-pituitary-adrenal (HPA) axis.

This reaction lasts longer, forcing your body to make bigger changes to prevent harm caused by ongoing stress. Imagine constantly hearing your smoke detector go off as little fires continually pop up. You would then likely take larger-scale action to not only put out multiple fires at once but also to prevent additional fires from being started again.

Unfortunately, your nervous system isn't very good at discriminating between short-term and long-term danger. It also can't often tell when a threat is physical or mental. Your body can react just as strongly if you're under a lot of stress over a heated dispute with a friend, a work deadline, or a stack of debts. The more your emergency stress system is engaged, the easier it becomes to activate later on and the more difficult it is to deactivate. This is why lots of short-term stressors can quickly add up to chronic stress.

Chronic Stress

If you never get a chance to relax and your body doesn't get a break from stress hormones, you may face serious mental and health challenges. Nearly every process in your body is disrupted by persistent stress. At first, it may lead to sadness, irritability, or anger. You may also feel lonely or overwhelmed. Over time, stress can put you at risk for developing conditions like anxiety, depression, and anxiety attacks. Stress can also make these experiences worse if you already experienced them. You may also notice that your sleep is disrupted. Perhaps you lie awake for a long time before falling asleep, or you wake up several times throughout the night.

Many people are tempted to deal with high stress levels in unhealthy ways such as alcohol or substance abuse, smoking cigarettes, overeating, undereating, going on unaffordable shopping sprees, or spending too much time watching television or scrolling through social media. You may have a harder time caring for yourself, exercising, or seeing loved ones. For some, chronic stress can lead to self-harm or even suicide.

You may also find that your mental functioning is impacted by stress. Some studies have found that ongoing exposure to stress hormones can shrink the brain, impact memory, and get in the way of your thinking skills. Over time, ongoing stress can change the way your brain is wired. For example, you may have trouble concentrating, feel like you can't process things as quickly as you should, or feel like your mind is in a fog. Stress can also make you feel very unmotivated to do things you need or want to do.

Ongoing stress also affects many different systems within your body, leading to changes in your physical health. If you have been dealing with stress, you may experience:

• Unusual tiredness or low energy levels

• Sleeping too much or too little

- Feelings of dizziness or lightheadedness
- Body aches or joint pains
- Nervous habits such as nail biting or pacing
- Clenched muscles
- A tightened jaw or teeth grinding
- Headaches
- Chest pain
- Heart palpitations (skipped heartbeats or a feeling like your heart is racing)
- Appetite changes or weight gain or loss
- Digestive symptoms like heartburn, nausea, abdominal cramps, diarrhea, or constipation
- Acne, eczema, or other skin symptoms
- More frequent infections, such as colds or the flu
- Changes in your menstrual period
- An increased or decreased sex drive

Chronic stress also increases your risk of developing ongoing medical conditions such as diabetes, hypertension (high blood pressure), heart disease, heart attacks, strokes, autoimmune conditions, eczema and other skin disorders, and infertility. It can also lead to more severe symptoms if you have conditions like asthma, chronic obstructive pulmonary disease (COPD), or irritable bowel syndrome (IBS). Because your body's stress response affects your immune system, you may have a higher risk of infections and other conditions that your immune cells are normally responsible for fighting off. Stressed-out people are even more likely to be diagnosed with cancer.

Decreasing the amount of stress in your life greatly enhances your overall health and may even increase your lifespan. Furthermore, stress and happiness rarely go together.

Reducing your stress levels will likely lead to greater joy and a stronger sense of purpose and well-being.

It's time to take action to rebalance your nervous system if you constantly feel stressed and overloaded. By becoming aware of the telltale signs and symptoms of chronic stress and taking preventative measures to lessen its negative effects, you may safeguard yourself and improve how you feel and think.

Fighting Stress with
the SHAPE Framework

"Stress is not what happens to us.
It's our response to what happens.
And response is something we can choose."

—Maureen Killoran

Stress management isn't regularly incorporated into academic curriculums, parenting handbooks, or work training programs. As a result, few of us realize that we can build up new tools that can help combat stress when it arises. There are skills that you can learn, practice, and adapt to your own situation. These practices are essential for maintaining physical and mental health and for building a life that allows you to get to where you want to be without being held back by worry and doubt.

Fighting Stress With the SHAPE Framework

I have developed the SHAPE framework as a way to help you design and achieve your ideal stress-free life. This process is partly based on my extensive research into how stress pathways work in our brains. It is also heavily influenced by my own experiences learning to manage stress, helping cancer patients and their caregivers find peace during incredibly stressful times, and guiding my clients in the Stress Blueprint Academy toward living their best lives. Because my nursing background taught me to approach problems with a scientific mindset, I have paired my stress-fighting program with evidence-based assessments to hone and perfect my approach to helping people manage stress.

My approach to stress management is rooted and adapted from a system used in the nursing profession. I realized I could also use this same systematic way of thinking when dealing with stress. I built the SHAPE framework as a way to guide you through a step-by-step approach to fighting stress as a part of your wellness journey.

Stress Management Involves Understanding Yourself

My experience has taught me that people don't often have the full picture when it comes to really understanding why they're stressed. Sure, some things are obvious, but it's easier than you may think to overlook sources of worry and anxiety. Minor stressors at work may feel like a bigger deal than they should because you're also carrying the weight of issues you haven't yet addressed at home.

I have found that stress management becomes a lot easier once you assess and acknowledge the full story of what's happening around you. What are all of the different factors that are impacting your life? You may need to dig deep to uncover all of the little facets that make up who you are and where you are at this moment in time. It also helps to better understand that your own perception of your stressors has a major influence on your current state of mind. I believe that asking yourself introspective questions about what's going on in your life is an important part of stress management.

Once you've taken the step of better understanding yourself, your environment, and your mindset, you can start thinking about where you want to be. During tough times, stress often clouds your thinking and overshadows your goals. By clarifying your values and intentions and allowing them to serve as your anchor, you can more easily refocus, cut through the stress, and take positive steps forward.

Does this seem daunting? I have found that many times, we already have many of the tools we need to gain the peaceful lives we desire. You can also gain new skills to reach your goals more easily than you might expect, as long as you have a solid plan of action and can identify helpful resources.

The SHAPE framework helps you accomplish all of this and more. It breaks down these ideas into simple, achievable steps that you can adapt to your situation. Through this book, I will help you operationalize your approach to stress management by walking you through a process for analyzing where you are now, defining the stress-free life-style that you want to reach in the future, and planning how you're going to get there.

FRAMEWORK *for* STRESS MANAGEMENT

Questions for Reflection

What are the biggest stressors in your life?

Which external factors are most likely to affect your mental health? What are the internal thoughts and beliefs that add to your mental load?

_____

_____

_____

_____

Do you remember a time when you experienced stress in a positive way?

Recall an occasion when stress was beneficial. Were you able to be more productive? Focus more clearly? Did you feel pride, a sense of accomplishment, or some other positive feeling once you were out of the stressful situation? Describe these thoughts and feelings.

_____

_____

_____

_____

Activity:
Recognize Stress in Your Mind and Body

Where in your body do you carry stress? Take time to pay attention to your thoughts and the way your body feels, and look for signs of stress. Set one or more alarms on a phone, watch, or clock, and check in with yourself when you hear the chime. Have you been spending a lot of time mindlessly looking at your phone? Are you having trouble focusing on important things? Is your jaw clenched? Does your stomach feel uneasy? Get used to recognizing how stress manifests itself in your body so you can learn to more effectively manage it when it arises.

STEP 1: Story

Who are you? How did you get to where you are now?

CHAPTER 1:

The Importance of Personal Introspection

"Real transformation requires real honesty.
If you want to move forward — get real with yourself."

—Bryant McGill

"God, my hips are huge!" exclaims Karen, one of the popular girls in the teen comedy movie Mean Girls.

"Oh please, I hate my calves," responds Gretchen, joining her friend in front of the mirror.

"At least you guys can wear halters," complains Regina, examining her arms in her reflection. "I've got man shoulders."

One by one, the three teens turn to look at Cady, the newest member of the group. It's clear she's expected to offer up critiques of her appearance. *I used to think there was just "fat" and "skinny,"* Cady thinks to herself. *Apparently, there are a lot of things that can be wrong with your body.*

What are the first few things you notice about yourself when you stand in front of the mirror?

Most likely, your eyes are immediately drawn toward your weight, hair, body, clothes, or other external elements. Starting from a young age, we learn to analyze our physical appearances with a critical eye.

But what about your inner appearance? How often do you stop and think about how your opinions, ideas, beliefs, and values shape who you are as a person? Most of us spend far more time analyzing our physical appearance than we do reflecting on our inner workings.

Although there may not be a physical mirror in which to see your true self, there is a mental one! "Self-reflection" refers to this mental mirror that enables you to examine your inner self and transform your life. This practice can be a crucial tool to transform your overall health and banish stress. When you make self-reflection a regular habit in your everyday routine and spend as much time on your inner self as you do looking in the mirror, your life is sure to change in positive ways.

What is Self-Reflection?

Self-reflection is a method of introspection and a strategy to look within oneself. It enables us to examine our internal and external circumstances. In other words, it's like holding a mirror up to your mind.

Without self-reflection, you may barrel forward down the same life path without stopping to think about whether there might be another route that can get you closer to where you want to be. You continue to find yourself in the middle of the same stressful situations and see and

hear yourself reacting in the same ways. You may feel like a hamster stuck on a spinning wheel; you're putting all of your effort towards staying on course, but you're not actually getting anywhere.

This cycle often leads to burnout and frequently does more harm than good. After all, according to Albert Einstein, "Insanity is doing the same thing over and over and expecting different results."

Self-reflection is the tool that can help you get off of that hamster wheel. It can help you identify how you reached your current location and visualize new paths forward. When you reflect on your thoughts, you can keep track of your development as a person.

Self-reflection is key when working through the SHAPE framework. You won't be able to reach a more peaceful existence and build the life you want for yourself if you don't truly understand the driving forces within your inner self.

How Can Self-Reflection Impact Your Life?

Self-reflection improves our lives in numerous ways. When you take the time to examine your mental mirror, you can:

- **Track your successes.** Unfortunately, our minds are more likely to hold on to the things we did wrong than the things we did right. We tend to think the worst of ourselves and expect failure in the future.

It may help to know that many incredibly successful people struggle with getting bogged down by negativity and self-doubt. "I feel every time I'm making a movie, I feel like [it's] my first movie.

Every time I have the same fear that I'm gonna be fired," said Penélope Cruz in an interview.

Famous writer, activist, and Nobel Laureate Maya Angelou once said, "I have written 11 books, but each time I think, 'Uh oh, they're going to find out now. I've run a game on everybody, and they're going to find me out.'" Even Leonardo Da Vinci, one of the most famous artists of all time, doubted his accomplishments: "Tell me if I ever did a thing," he wrote in his diary one day.

However, when you are honest about who you are and what you've done, you'll see not only some failures but also some shining victories. Self-reflection helps you acknowledge what you've done right and use those to fuel new successes. When you're in a tough situation, you can focus on what you've done well in the past.

- **Allow your relationships to flourish.** By considering how you treat others, you can build more peaceful, meaningful connections with other people.

When you reflect on yourself, you can better comprehend how you feel about the people around you and recognize the benefits of various relationships in your life. This can make you feel more grateful for those in your family or close circle of friends. Additionally, showing gratitude for your loved ones can help deepen your relationships with them.

- **Get better sleep.** We frequently have regrets and unresolved issues swirling around our minds when we go to bed, which interferes with a good night's rest. In fact, worries and repetitive thoughts are some of the most common causes of poor sleep.

It is through self-reflection that we are able to identify and work through our unresolved emotions. By practicing reflection, we are able to avoid falling victim to the cycle of rumination.

As a result, we sleep longer, and our sleep is more restful.

- **Reduce your anxiety and stress levels.** Self-reflection exercises make you feel more rooted in the present and put you in touch with your senses.

Imagine that you're driving a motorcycle for the first time. You don't entirely know what you're doing, and you're not feeling very comfortable. Your mind is fully engaged in the present moment. You're looking at the road in front of you, listening to the sound of the engine, and putting all your focus into stepping on the right pedals and moving your body in the right ways.

You don't have the mental space to feel bad about something that happened yesterday or worry about what tomorrow might bring.

Self-reflection can put you in a similar state. You're living in the present and focusing on your current inner self rather than ruminating on past mistakes or agonizing over future what-ifs.

There's less room for tension, stress, and anxiety in your mind.

- **Be more creative.** Some research has found that self-reflection can sometimes boost creativity. While being overly critical of yourself or judging every step of your work can sometimes hinder creative thoughts, healthy self-reflection can allow good ideas to float to the top.

Just as not every plant that grows in your garden is wanted, not all of your creative thoughts or efforts will turn into great achievements. Weeding your garden gives more room for beautiful flowers to grow, and self-reflection allows you to let go of unhelpful ideas to make room for the ones that will be the most successful.

- **Experience greater clarity.** As you become more conscious of the deepest parts of your being, your thoughts become clearer.

Self-reflection can be like the process of putting together a jigsaw puzzle. As you stare down at hundreds of tiny little pieces, you may initially feel unsure of where to start. The individual pieces don't tell any sort of story on their own. However, you soon start to find connections. You find puzzle pieces that match, realize how groups of connected pieces fit together, and eventually, the big picture emerges.

Likewise, when you engage in self-reflection, you may at first see a lot of separate puzzle pieces—different roles, ideas, goals, beliefs, and memories—. Still, it may not be clear exactly how each part led you to where you are now. However, when you keep engaging with your inner mind, you'll soon start to find links. Your mental fog will begin to clear, and you'll have a more accurate picture of yourself that can help you better understand and use your motivations.

Self-Awareness Unlocks Your Capacity for Living Stress-Free

How self-aware are you? Who are you without all of your titles and roles? What is your vision? What are your stress triggers? It's not always pleasant to discover more about yourself, but it's necessary if you want to effectively manage your stressors and develop sustainable stress solutions.

Self-awareness is the key to recognizing, understanding, and regulating your emotions and stressors. When you lack self-awareness, your perception of reality is blurred, like walking through the world with dilated eyes. If you do not know who you are, how can you recognize the reasons behind your emotions? How can you plan out what your next steps should be?

One important step in developing self-awareness is getting clarity on your values. Think of what's truly important in your life. What brings you a sense of purpose, and what are things that define who you are as an individual? Take a few minutes to list your top three values that represent who you are and what you believe at this very moment in your life.

It's also important to be aware of your goals. It's easy to fall into the trap of living aimlessly, letting things happen around us without taking an active role in intentionally shaping our actions.

However, when you know your goals, you can gain a better understanding of what or who you need in your life and act accordingly to accomplish your goals.

You can learn a lot about yourself by intentionally paying attention and checking in with yourself. I want you to be cautious not to judge yourself in the moment; instead, take note of what you are feeling and explore the why behind the feeling. Notice any stressors and your reactions to them. Also, pay attention to when you feel especially relaxed, content, or peaceful.

What factors are leading to these emotions and sensations? Pick a day each week to capture your stressors and your reactions to them. Alternatively, choose certain time points during the day to check in with yourself and document your thoughts, feelings, and attitudes that are most prominent within that particular moment. Revisit the situations that triggered negative emotions and imagine what you could have done to change the impact the situation had on you. I want to remind you that you cannot control other people. You can only control yourself and your reactions.

Recording your observations in a journal, computer document, or journaling app can be a great way to help you get your thoughts in order and allow you to go back and reflect on what you were going through. Keeping and updating a record of your emotions is an easy, effective way to build more awareness and understanding of yourself.

Once you have gotten into the habit of writing down your thoughts, feelings, and activities, do a comprehensive assessment of the data you collected. There are many factors you may want to consider. How did you spend your time? What did you enjoy? What did you dislike? Did you lose your temper? If so, why? What was the best thing that happened to you?

What was so great about it? What was the worst thing that happened? What would you change about the day? What did you learn about yourself today? How did you do in your relationship?

What did you learn about your partner? What could you have done better? Do you feel like you are coming to better understand your vision, purpose, and gifts?

Getting to know yourself better can help you cut through the stress. It helps you cut through all the temporary stressors swirling around you while clarifying who you are deep down.

While stressors can quickly come and go, your answers to these introspective questions often remain more constant.

Building a Self-Reflection Practice

You can use the amazing tool of self-reflection in various ways to transform your life. One of the most important things to keep in mind is that self-reflection is not something you do once. It is an ongoing, lifelong practice. You are constantly growing, and your environment and circumstances regularly undergo change, so even if you feel like you know yourself well now, there may be more to uncover a year, a month, or even a week from now. Try to make self-reflection a regular habit through some of the following strategies:

- **Ask yourself the four W and one H questions.** This is undoubtedly among the best methods for engaging in daily self-reflection.

You need to develop a practice of addressing the following: Who am I? What do I want? Where do I want to be?

Why is this important to me? How am I going to get there? Turn these questions inward and focus your answers on the current moment. Don't think about the person you used to be ten years ago or the place you want to be in the future. Answer these questions in the here and now to get an accurate snapshot that serves as your current starting point for change.

Keep in mind that this is an ongoing process. As you develop, grow, and learn more about yourself, keep looking inward at your mental mirror and assessing the four Ws and one H at each given moment.

- **Jot everything down.** Writing down your ideas and feelings is always a good approach to channeling and gaining control over them. You can begin journaling as a daily exercise in self-reflection. It will also enable you to monitor your life's progress.

One good way to practice journaling is to choose a question to answer in your journal each Saturday morning once you first wake up. Once you have this habit down, try journaling a couple of times per week or even every day.

Some questions to start your practice include: How do I feel in my body right now? What three things increased my stress levels in the past week, and why? What actions or activities tend to bring me peace? What are my current stress management practices, and how well is each one working? Which fears are currently holding me back from putting myself forward? How would I feel and act if I fully believed I was capable of being successful in my current situation?

Being honest with yourself can be very challenging. It doesn't always feel good to think back on negative memories or to acknowledge flaws within ourselves. However, pushing through and being willing to do the work will get you results. I promise you that you can transform your life if you're willing to do the work.

CHAPTER 2

Writing Your Story

"There is no greater agony than bearing an untold story inside you."

—Maya Angelou

How do you perceive yourself? What do other people think of you? And who are you truly, deep down?

These three identities were in conflict when COVID-19 shifted my personal and professional life. For me, as for many others, the pandemic was a turning point that required me to rely on deep-seated internal reserves. Finding that extra source of strength within myself was like reaching all the way in the back of the closet for that box of shoes preserved in dust.

The Power of Your Story

Prior to the pandemic, I was a decisive nurse leader. I was confident, and I had influence in my profession. At the time, I worked as a Clinical Scientist from the comfort of my home. I was also a new mom to a beautiful baby boy, Claude II.

His arrival into this world had me reevaluate my life. He helped fill an emptiness I had been carrying for the past couple of years. I now realize that that emptiness was a yearning for patient contact after leaving clinical nursing to enter the pharmaceutical sector of healthcare. I longed to be back at the bedside. I missed connecting with patients and knowing that I could positively impact their lives. I had prided myself on being able to help patients manage their mental health and see their situations from a different perspective as they struggled through their treatments. Still, I felt like something was missing from my life. Although "mom" was an exciting new role for me, it highlighted how much I felt something was missing from my professional life.

When COVID-19 hit, my identities were further confused. Was it time to switch careers?

Was now a good time to go back to seeing patients in person? What about my newly growing family? At this point in my life, more than ever, I felt the need to figure out what life story I wanted to tell.

Your story is a compilation of all the things that have happened to you so far. It paints a picture of where you currently are in life and how you got there. It is like a roadmap that describes the path you are on and the destination you are walking towards.

Telling your story during stressful times creates distance between you and your stressors. Framing your experience as an ongoing adventure allows you to:

- Be aware of what you've been through.
- Assess what happened and analyze your ideal outcomes.
- Reassess and align your values.
- Develop an action-oriented mindset that helps you understand how best to move forward.

There is power in having full awareness of what you are going through and to name the stressors that are occurring in your life. Think through your stressors. How long have they been happening? Are they external or internal? In other words, how much control do you have over them? What impacts do your stressors have on various aspects of your life?

We Grow During Tough Choices

There are a few key moments when we come to pivotal points in our lives, like a one-way narrow road that splits into multiple directions, where we have to make decisions that will propel us toward our next destination. When we arrive at that intersection, the choices can be overwhelming. Do I go straight, left, or right?

Before becoming a Clinical Scientist, I worked as a Medical Science Liaison (MSL). This job involved developing relationships with Key Oncology Opinion Leaders, which many know as cancer care providers, and discussing new and existing clinical trials that could help their patients. As a part of this role, I recall visiting a cancer center in Connecticut. I walked onto the unit full of nostalgia. The smell of medical disinfectant, the sounds of the infusion pumps beeping, and the sight of patients and nurses conversing felt like home. Unfortunately, however, I wasn't visiting to help patients.

I was ushered into a conference room to speak with the healthcare providers about clinical trials. As I was giving the presentation on the extensive clinical trial pipeline, the only thing I could think about was asking the question, "Can I tour the infusion center?"

After the presentation, the staff was happy to give me a tour. I eagerly stood up and walked towards the door, instantly feeling a sense of joy. I walked around the infusion center with a huge smile on my face and pride in my soul as I greeted the nearest nurse. She was decked out in green scrubs, getting ready to administer a bag of saline to a patient sitting in a recliner wearing blue jeans and a pink and blue checkered shirt with a rose-colored bonnet covering her bald head. I was ready to return to the clinic right at that very moment. However, I first had to figure out whether a career switch was the next chapter of my story.

Ultimately, I decided to explore returning to the clinical setting on an as-needed basis in January 2020. After interviewing and getting excited about the possibilities of getting back to a job that made my heart sing, the COVID-19 pandemic hit. Then, it happened: I checked my email and found a job offer for an Outpatient Hematology Oncology Advanced Practice Registered Nurse clinical nursing role. The words "We understand if you do not accept due to the pandemic" jumped off the screen.

My heart raced, and questions flooded my brain like a rogue wave engulfing a ship. *What are you going to do now? I thought to myself. Do you want to compromise the health of your family, especially your new baby? What will people think if you accept the position while being a new mom?* And, one of the biggest questions of all: *There is a virus killing people. How could you even consider going back to the hospital?*

At that moment, standing in the kitchen holding my cell phone, I felt that my superhero cape was torn between being a good mother and an honorable healthcare provider. The uneasiness that wore on my soul was caused by that thing, that awful feeling in the pit of my stomach, the thing that kept me up at night, the thing that occupied my thoughts, the thing called PURPOSE! It would not allow me to rest. I stewed, pondered, and stressed over this crossroad. In the meantime, the COVID-19 pandemic cracked through my shell of confidence, decisiveness, and strength. It exposed my underlying emotions and thoughts, leaving me with the eerie and unshakeable feeling of standing in the window naked and exposed.

When you come to those big crossroads, the most important part of keeping your story moving forward is not which path you choose. It is simply taking action and making any choice at all.

We have to move. Stress can paralyze us, leaving us stuck in place. Extreme worry about a situation can rob you of your power to choose and grow. If you stay still too long, you may even lose momentum and backtrack along the path you had been traveling.

Ultimately, it may not even matter much which direction you choose. You will win by gaining a new experience or failing forward, both of which can enhance your strength. This process can be stressful, but it leads to growth.

Is Your Story Written By You or By Others?

At times, we ignore our gut feeling to listen to ourselves. You may ignore the little voice inside your head or the yearnings of your heart and put more effort into trying to align with external societal norms.

While this behavior is tempting, it doesn't fully honor your experience and your story. That gut feeling you sometimes push away is your subconscious mind knocking on the door of your conscious mind. When ignored, this feeling can transform into an internal stressor that takes over your mind and hinders your ability to live fully out in the world.

It was March 2020, and we were in the beginning stages of lockdown. I was sitting paralyzed on the fluffy gray microfiber loveseat couch, breastfeeding my newborn son while wearing my metaphorical torn superhero cape. My new husband was sitting on the couch next to me, and my elderly mother was perched on the edge of the sofa, clutching the remote control with wide eyes. Together, we watched the number of COVID-19 deaths increase on television.

Externally, I'm sure I seemed strong, happy, and unbothered despite the alarming news.

Internally, however, my heart was beating fast, and my stomach was in knots. I was riddled with fear, nervousness, and stress. I looked down at my precious son, who was latched onto my left breast, and then looked up at the news on the television screen. All I could think about were the people and families represented by the increasing numbers on the screen. As my head bowed, my right leg shook, and my lip gradually became chapped due to my frequent biting, I thought about the woman from the infusion center, sitting in her recliner with her rose-colored bonnet. I remembered so many of the other patients and families that I had cared for throughout my career. How were they holding up? How were they affected by all of these sudden changes, by this virus that was claiming so many lives? Was I right to want to get back to the clinic to help?

Right in the middle of this thought, my mother interrupted like a horn playing in the library. "I am so happy that you are not working in the hospital," she said in a matter-of-fact tone.

As I looked into her wide, fearful eyes, I felt my entire body sink into the sofa. I forced my head to nod, signaling that I agreed with her, even as I felt confusion and doubt taking over.

We lose a sense of control during stressful times. We say and do things we do not necessarily agree with. We may follow the crowd rather than striking out on our own. But this can lead to harmful results. It's like your mom probably scolded you: "If all of your friends jumped off a cliff, would you?"

Research has shown that our unconscious state influences our waking mind, allowing stress to impact our ability to reason and think critically. When stress grows, we often enter a cycle in which we hand over our power to the stressor like a puppet controlled by a ventriloquist.

This can cause our feelings of strain to grow and even spill over into other aspects of our lives, holding us back in many areas. To regain control over our lives, we must first learn to conquer the stress.

Allowing Your Story To Guide Your Life

Of course, my mother was nervous about COVID-19. She was an elderly adult with comorbidities with a high risk of death if she contracted the virus. My husband was less concerned. He sat on the couch next to me, looking unbothered, scrolling through email on his cell phone with his thumb.

Me? I was conflicted. COVID-19 was actively killing people on a global scale. However, at my core, I knew that there was something I could do to help. I had the ability to contribute. Hell, I was trained for this. It's the reason I became a nurse.

The inklings of unsettled yearning began to rise in me. I had subconsciously suppressed these feelings for years, but I was suddenly presented with an opportunity to fill the hole growing inside of me. I could have pushed down those thoughts and continued about my days in a more comfortable position, but my life's purpose had other plans. I longed to return to the frontline as a nurse and serve cancer patients.

As I continued to sit and watch the news, I was riddled with stress and fear. At the time, I felt like I really didn't know what to do, but in retrospect, I can see that I was wrestling with my purpose. I ached for it. I was compelled by it. I could not shake this feeling because it was my purpose manifesting—the reason I exist in this world. Yet, at the same time, I had good reason to doubt whether these feelings would lead me down the right path. How could I risk my family's health as a new mom who was now responsible for this new life? How could I risk my mother's disappointment when I knew that my staying out of the hospital was a source of comfort for her?

Then, BOOM, out of nowhere, while sitting on the same gray loveseat with my head back and eyes closed, I heard my late grandfather's words. *"In this chapter of your life, you have to set your sail."* That was it. That was the catalyst. Those words mended my torn cape and allowed me to fly. Despite the pandemic, despite being a new mother, and despite my mother's dismay, I decided to return to the frontlines to serve cancer patients. That one decision literally freed me.

Sometimes, we have a tendency to allow stress, uncertainty, and fear to shackle us like prisoners. Stressing about the unknown can keep you from aligning with your purpose and living in your truth.

On the other hand, keeping your story in mind can help keep you moving down the path you want to be on. It can free you from the prison of fear created by your stressors. In every moment of every day, you are shaping your individual story. A single decision can change the trajectory of your entire life.

Stress management requires us to make an intentional decision to manage our lives. You need to get in the driving seat and take the wheel back from your stressors while you wave goodbye in the rearview mirror. That ONE decision to start actively shaping your own life can open the door to endless and unimaginable possibilities that we may not even realize are possible.

Questions for Reflection

What are some of your main stressors?

What are the things that are weighing most heavily on your mind? What is keeping you up at night? List several of the stressors keeping you up at night.

_____

_____

_____

_____

What impact do your stressors have on your life?

Pick one stressor and think through it carefully. When did it begin? Does it have an internal or external source? Which parts of your life are affected by the presence of this stressor?

_____

_____

_____

_____

Do you remember a time you ignored your gut feeling and did not truly honor yourself?

Think back to an occasion in which you followed the crowd or took someone else's advice despite having an inkling that it wasn't the right move for you. How did you feel at the time? What was the impact of this decision? In hindsight, have your feelings or thoughts changed on the matter?

_____

_____

_____

_____

Have you ever struggled to make a big decision?

Think about a time when you were at the crossroads of life and felt stuck by a decision lying in front of you. What was on the other side of that decision? Even if it didn't turn out like you expected, what did you gain from making a choice?

_____

_____

_____

_____

What is your main purpose? Thinking back to your life story, what is one thing that really lights up your life? What type of work, activity, or hobby do you feel truly defines what's important to you? Why were you put on this earth?

_____

_____

_____

_____

Activity:
Start Drafting Your Life Story

Before you panic, don't worry, I'm not asking you to crank out a best-selling memoir. This is just for you, unless you later decide to share it with someone. Let's start small:

- Buy a small notebook, gather a few sheets of paper, or open up a document on your computer.

- Next, start to write. Put your story on the page. It doesn't have to contain perfect spelling or make sense to anyone else but you. Think about the major stressors you have faced and make a list.

- Now, rank your stressors. Which one seems to be weighing most heavily on you at this moment? What's your number 2 stressor, and so on?

- For each stressor, write down how it is impacting your life. How does it influence your physical, mental, emotional, social, occupational, and spiritual wellness? Are you in control of this situation? Is it an internal or external stressor? How is it showing up in your life? Start creating a basic story explaining who you are, the obstacles you've overcome, and the ones you're currently facing.

- Over time, continue to add to your story or occasionally pull it out to read it and put your current struggles into perspective.

STEP 2: Hone

Can you pinpoint where you want to go next?
What are your next steps?

CHAPTER 3:

Practicing Mindfulness

"The present moment is the only time over
which we have dominion."

—Thich Nhat Hanh

On a recent spring day, I took my three-year-old son to the park. I hadn't been to a park in many years, but we had a free morning, so I seized the opportunity. I didn't even bring my phone along. It was just him and me going up the little ladders, going down the slides, and working our way across the monkey bars. I was transported back to my childhood as I saw my peace and happiness reflected in his ear-to-ear grin.

This experience was what I like to call a "golden moment"—a moment in which your mind is fully engaged in a wonderful experience that you know you're going to remember fondly for the rest of your life. To create these moments, you must be keenly aware of everything happening around you.

I've long known that mindfulness is an important stress-fighting tool, but golden moments with my son have helped me more fully embrace the practice of staying in the moment. He helps me remember to be present with him as much as possible. After all, I don't want to miss any once-in-a-lifetime milestones with him!

Whatever stage of life you are currently in, mindfulness has the power to improve it. In particular, people frequently turn to mindfulness meditation in trying circumstances, such as during a divorce or breakup, after losing a loved one, after receiving a serious sickness diagnosis, or when their lives are very stressful.

Practicing mindfulness during these times can allow us to escape the chaos of life, even for just a moment. It can help alleviate suffering, uncertainty, and heartbreak. Contrary to popular belief, this meditation technique also shows us how to overcome challenges in life rather than avoid them. Mindfulness forces us to softly and reassuringly engage our fears and concerns rather than run away from challenging situations. The remedy we sorely need now is mindfulness, centering on the here and now and not being afraid of the ideas and emotions we encounter. But it's also the one we tend to avoid when we turn to apps, TV, and other distractions.

What Is Mindfulness?

Without a doubt, you have seen references to "mindfulness." This term can pop up virtually anywhere, including in books, periodicals, blog postings, YouTube videos, and more. This and other forms of mindfulness can be seen in movies ranging from *Star Wars* to *The Karate Kid*.

Still, many individuals are unaware of what mindfulness training actually entails.

People frequently think mindfulness involves practicing Buddhism or is only for very spiritual people. This is sometimes true. However, at its core, mindfulness is a really basic idea. You can do it whenever and wherever.

Mindfulness means being aware of your feelings, thoughts, and physical sensations, as well as the things happening around you, while keeping your attention on the present moment.

Mindfulness is the opposite of mindlessness. The term "mindless" is frequently used to describe thoughtless or detached acts. It's typically employed when someone acts carelessly.

Many people spend a significant portion of their days mindlessly because they are not paying attention to the present moment and are instead thinking about the past or the future.

Mindfulness, on the other hand, involves fully engaging with where you're at in the moment.

Think about how frequently you are preoccupied with the past or the future. Do you ever find yourself wondering what you're going to do when a business meeting is over? Are you planning what to wear on a night out or daydreaming about the delectable lunch you'll eat that afternoon? Are you reflecting on the event you attended last week or thinking about your performance on the last test?

You may focus on the task at hand for brief periods throughout the day, but these moments are frequently fleeting. You may have noticed that your mind tends to wander more often than it concentrates. This isn't necessarily terrible. But over time, it can be detrimental, and it's frequently worse when we are unaware that our minds are wandering. It's like trying to hold on to a handful of sand; the tighter you squeeze, the more grains of sand escape.

To stop the mind from wandering, you can practice mindfulness regularly. This will help you get better at staying in the present moment. Mindfulness can enhance your focus and memory, as well as assist you in becoming a better listener. These abilities will be helpful if you are in school or have a job that is extremely hard.

The physical advantages of mindfulness extend to the body. Mindfulness has been associated with pain reduction for chronic illnesses such as lower back pain, fibromyalgia, and other musculoskeletal pain. As stress and anxiety decrease, mental and emotional health also improve. This may help protect you from mental health issues like depression. Better sleep has also been connected to mindfulness. Finally, research has demonstrated that mindfulness can enhance and support the immune system.

No matter your religion, denomination, or whether you follow another spiritual philosophy, you can practice mindfulness and gain its benefits. Simply put, mindfulness is a way of being.

Buddhist Teachings on Mindfulness

If you want to understand how mindfulness entered the West, you need to go back more than 2,600 years to when the Buddha attained enlightenment and began to impart the value of mindfulness to others.

Siddhartha Gautama, the Buddha, described mindfulness as "the way to enlightenment." He requested that his senior monks, known as bhikkhus, teach a doctrine known as The Four Foundations of Mindfulness in order to teach others about their practices. These foundations were:

- To truly understand the body, spend some time in-depth, dwelling, fully grasping, and focused contemplation of the body within the body.
- Spend some time dwelling on your feelings in order to understand them for what they truly are.
- Spend some time dwelling on your mind in order to understand it more fully.

- Understand dhammas for what they truly are. (The Buddha uses the term "dhamma" to refer to phenomena, or the sum of a person's experiences, which includes all mental events that constantly arise within us)

Each of the Four Foundations of Mindfulness is typically viewed as a stage in an overall process of mastering perfect present-moment awareness. The first step is to concentrate on body awareness. You can start by simply concentrating on your breath—simply notice what it feels like as your lungs fill and deflate or pay attention to the sensation of air entering or leaving your nose. Once you have mastered this, start paying attention to other sensations in your body.

Furthermore, through the practice of mindfulness, feelings are thoroughly investigated. This encompasses sentiments, emotions, and any bodily sensations accompanying them. You will pay attention to any thoughts you have. Simply notice them, acknowledge them, and then let them pass.

Observing without passing judgment is one of the cornerstones of practicing mindfulness.

You need to learn to let the sensations, feelings, and thoughts flow through you without trying to "fix" them, change them, or do anything about them. Simply let them be present.

It's harder than you might imagine. For instance, your thoughts can stray while you're attempting to be mindful. You might begin to recall a recent argument you had with your significant other. You may start to experience rage, grief, and frustration as a result. Even if you're attempting to pay attention to your breathing, your thoughts will move in other directions, and you may be tempted to judge or ignore them. However, the objective is not to ignore thoughts, feelings, or other senses. Instead, you should acknowledge them and then turn your attention back to your original goal.

To get an idea of what a mindfulness practice should be like, picture driving down a street. Your attention may occasionally be captured by something happening outside. For example, you notice a new billboard, a person walking on the sidewalk, or an unusually-colored car. Most of the time, you won't think deeply about any of these extra things that you see. You simply notice them and then return your focus back to your driving.

The Benefits of Mindfulness

Science has repeatedly proven that practicing mindfulness will improve your health, strength, wisdom, and calmness.

When you start regularly going through mindfulness exercises, you may notice:

- **Growth in mental health.** In 2015, 16.1 million Americans reported having depression, according to Harvard researchers. Although there are many types of therapy, like medication and cognitive behavioral therapy, not all patients benefit from these treatments.

On the other hand, a growing body of evidence shows that mindfulness positively impacts mental health, helping combat these mental health challenges.

- **Reduced anxiety and stress.** A 2013 study from Massachusetts General Hospital found that a stress reduction program based on mindfulness practices helped people experience less anxiety.

Better mental abilities. Research has also found that practicing mindfulness leads to an increase in gray matter in the brain. This may be linked to IQ gains, enhanced attention and concentration, and increased communication abilities.

- **Better physical health.** A 2018 study found that even just fifteen minutes a day of mindfulness practice lowered participants' blood pressure. People who practiced mindfulness meditation regularly for more than eight weeks also had more efficient metabolism, less inflammation, and better sleep patterns.

Some mindfulness exercises also incorporate physical activity. This can provide extra benefits for your mental and physical health at the same time.

- **Reduction in pain.** Some research has found that people experience less pain when they practice mindfulness. This can work for multiple types of pain, including ongoing chronic pain.

Beginning a Mindfulness Practice

Adopting a mindfulness practice is easier than you might think. Many people are under the impression that practicing mindfulness will take endless amounts of time. However, this isn't the case. You can start right now, right away! It's never too late to start. All it takes is making the decision to begin.

For a simple way to get started, take five days and follow this mindfulness schedule:

- **Day 1:** Spend five minutes enjoying the taste and texture of one food item. What are some creative words you can use to describe its taste? What does the food feel like in your mouth?

- **Day 2:** Spend five minutes identifying, isolating, and describing two sounds in your environment. Where are they coming from? Do they remind you of any other sounds? Describe them, being as specific as possible.

- **Day 3:** Spend five minutes touching and observing the texture of three items in your environment. Notice the objects' textures, temperatures, or weights.

- **Day 4:** Spend five minutes smelling four food items in your kitchen cabinet. Sit with each smell for a while, noticing the sensations it elicits.

- **Day 5:** Spend five minutes looking for five green items in your environment. How else can you describe what these items look like? Are they shiny? Dull? Patterned? What exact shade of green are they?

If you like, you can practice being mindful every day. In Buddhist teaching, mindfulness is a discipline; in essence, everything is awareness. Your complete focus should be on whatever you are doing, whether it is cooking, doing laundry, playing with your kids, writing a report for school, or simply going on a walk. Put all your focus into your current activity without multitasking. When you notice that your mind has started to wander, bring it back to the present moment by closing your eyes and refocusing on the present.

You can practice mindfulness during the simplest task, such as folding a batch of freshly washed and dried towels. Here's how you could use this chance to engage in some mindfulness:

- **Only focus on one task at a time.** A good place to start is by deciding to fold only laundry. While performing this task, turn off the TV and the music. Do not converse with anyone else while folding. Put all of your energy into folding this one load of laundry as well as you can.

- **Move slowly and with deliberateness.** Don't feel the need to fold everything right away. Because this is all you're doing right now, it demands your undivided attention. Exercise caution when moving and acting. Make sure the towels' corners are neatly aligned. Fold your towels neatly into matching types of stacks. Lint can be removed and piled up.

- **Take in the activity.** Enjoy yourself and what you're doing. Have the towels recently been in the dryer, making them warm and inviting? Your fingertips will be covered in warm fibers. Keep them close to your cheek. Sense how cleanly your washing detergent smells. Take pleasure in gathering all of the towels into a tidy stack that is ready for your linen closet.

- **Return to the task when your mind wanders.** Unavoidably, you'll start to daydream about what you'll do later that evening, how your current towels need to be replaced since they are worn out, or what you'd rather be doing than folding towels. That's all right! Once again, the objective is to simply become aware of your mind wandering, tell yourself where it is going (for instance, say out loud, "I'm thinking about what to have for dinner today," and then bring your attention back to the present and what you are doing, which is folding laundry). There are also many other ways to make mindfulness a habit. You can include the following things in your daily life to increase this practice:

- **Music that is calming or soothing.** Whenever possible, listen to soothing or tranquil music. Many of us are emotionally affected by music, and it can help us become calmer and more relaxed.

- **Relaxation videos.** Watching peaceful videos can be a great way to unwind and unwind. You can find free videos online or use mindfulness apps.

- Children's **mindfulness activities.** Try to engage your kids in kid-friendly mindful activities like mindful walks or mindful coloring. There is mindfulness available for teenagers who are dealing with the stress of peer pressure and school, so it's not only for the little ones.

- **Mindful movement.** You can practice attentive movements at home or when you're out and about. Go slowly and easily. Focus on the way that your body is moving. If possible, do this a few times per week.

- **Go on a walk.** Walking mindfully is a great way to practice walking meditation, whether you do it by yourself, with a partner, or with your kids. Enjoy every second, focus, put your phone away, and be totally present. One name for this practice is "forest bathing," and it significantly lowers stress and anxiety.

- **Mindful eating.** Practice mindfulness during mealtime by paying close attention to what you put in your mouth and how. Many things will benefit from mindful eating.

- **Stay away from screens.** Start being more aware of your surroundings: Don't be the person who rushes through life while glued to their phone. Start being more aware of your surroundings and making mindfulness a regular practice has countless advantages.

- **Make decisions with mindfulness.** When faced with a choice, make sure it's one made with mindfulness rather than in a hurry or without consideration. Stop everything else you're doing and put all of your focus toward your decision.

CHAPTER 4

Hone In on What You Want

"Where there is no vision, there is no hope."

—George Washington Carver

We are honored to welcome the next presenter, a Board Certified Nurse Practitioner, Stress Solution Strategist, Emotional Intelligence Consultant, international speaker, number one best-selling author, certified John Maxwell Coach and Trainer, with more than twenty years in the healthcare industry! She is the CEO of The Stress Blueprint and SHAPE Partners, creator of the Stress Blueprint Academy and Stress Solution Series, and host of the Nurse Wellness Podcast. This presenter has been featured in various print and televised media to further her message to impact more lives. She wants every opportunity to empower people to manage stress so people can optimize their overall well-being and align with their purpose. I introduce to you, Wendy Garvin Mayo!

I sat in the audience, frozen in my seat with wide eyes like someone injected me with a paralytic. This has certainly not always been my introduction.

I think back to when I was a child growing up in the inner city of Boston, surrounded by drugs and violence, being raised by a single mother. It was hard to see a clear vision of what my life could look like.

It was during the summer of 1992 when, for the first time, I captured an idea of what I wanted for my life. On a hot, humid Thursday night, I sat on the floor with my back pressed against my mother's queen-sized bed. My brother sat next to me with a cup of hot chocolate glued to his lips as his eyes peered over the top of the cup. We were watching *The Cosby Show* on our 19-inch color television, and I was completely enamored with Claire Huxtable. She wore matching skirt suits with nylon stockings, carried a brown leather briefcase, and when she came home from work, she was greeted by her physician husband and smart children. She seemed so happy.

From that day forward, whenever people asked me what I was going to be when I grew up, I would enthusiastically answer that I was going to be a lawyer. I didn't even understand what that meant, but I knew I wanted to be Claire Huxtable. Having her as my role model subconsciously motivated me to do well academically. I was the child who did not need an alarm clock or my mom to wake me up for school. I was up, dressed, and out the door every morning in time to catch the bus.

Each week, on Thursday at eight p.m. Eastern Standard Time, I would be in position in front of our TV to watch *The Cosby Show*. These weekly viewings fed my vision of hope and allowed me to escape the reality of the police sirens that echoed around my neighborhood. This vision kept me grounded since I knew that a college education was my ticket that would take me from Brunswick Street to Birchwood Road. Honing in on my vision motivated me to stay on track in school and helped me fulfill the accomplishments that now fill the introduction that is read out before I get on stage to speak or train. Although I never became a lawyer, I fulfilled the spirit of my vision by becoming a servant leader who empowers people to hone in on their goals and find clarity surrounding their purpose.

The Importance of Vision

Stress can lead to the loss of our life's vision. Without sight, it's hard to have clarity surrounding our purpose.

In this case, vision is the ability to plan or think about the future with imagination or wisdom. When stressed, negative feelings cloud your vision like shades keeping the sun out of a dark room. Honing in on your vision can help motivate you to manage your stressors even though you may currently be very far from where you want to be.

While the first step of the SHAPE framework—story—is all about exploring the past factors, both positive and negative that brought you to your current place in life, the next step—hone—is all about focusing on the vision of where you want to be in the future. It involves taking back your power from your stressors and refocusing your energy on your vision.

Practicing this framework step empowers you to visualize yourself to show up in the world as you want to be seen.

For inspiration, look no further than Beyoncé. Early on in her career, she created her own alter ego—a fun, sexy, glamorous, outspoken character named Sasha Fierce. Stepping into the shoes of a character helped her take more risks and perform to the best of her ability when she doubted her true self. Sasha Fierce "takes over when it's time for me to work and when I'm onstage," Beyoncé said. "[She's] this alter ego that I've created that kind of protects me and who I really am." In other words, she dreamed up a vision of who she wanted to be and took steps toward becoming that person.

Focusing on the vision of your ideal future amid stress comes down to mindset. Mindset is the established set of beliefs that you hold. It is essential that you take time to think about the root of your beliefs, as they shape the way you approach learning and reaching for your goals.

How Your Mindset Can
Set You Up for Success — Or Failure

Dr. Carol Dweck, a psychologist at Stanford University, coined the term "mindset" after she and her colleagues noticed that students tended to respond to stress in dramatically different ways.

Some of the students were incredibly distressed when they encountered minor hurdles. They didn't see the point in putting in extra effort and quickly gave up when the going got tough.

However, other students quickly got back on their feet after a failure, more determined than ever to overcome obstacles. They seemed to relish a good challenge. Dr. Dweck proposed that these contrasting beliefs and responses reflected different mindsets.

Dr. Dweck has spent decades studying the impact of mindset on behavior. Her theory is that your mindset helps describe the reasons we do or do not do certain things. She identified two different types of mindsets. People with **fixed mindsets** believe that changing or learning new skills is difficult or impossible. They are more likely to ignore useful feedback, avoid challenges, and stay away from new or unfamiliar things. To these individuals, things simply are the way they are. There is no other way, and there's no sense in trying to exert change. For those with fixed mindsets, the saying "You can't teach an old dog new tricks" rings true.

The opposite of a fixed mindset is a **growth mindset**. People who adopt this style of thinking tend to have more open minds. They are more willing to learn and try new things. A growth mindset encourages people to persist in the face of struggles and approach problems with an open mind. These individuals tend to be open to learning from criticism and enthusiastic about developing new skills because they believe these strategies will help them succeed. They are more likely to believe that success does not just happen. It is something that comes following hard work. People with growth mindsets often embrace challenges because they know trials will stretch them and help them develop.

The great news is that you can change your mindset. If you naturally tend to approach obstacles with a fixed mindset, you can eventually embrace a growth mindset that allows you to adapt to change and find success. Reading this book shows an openness to change.

A key part of evolving your mindset is understanding that things in your brain aren't fixed in place. Your brain cells are all connected in a complicated series of networks, but these networks constantly change throughout your life in a process called brain plasticity. Research shows that as you take in new experiences, your neurons form new connections and build new pathways.

In other words, your brain physically changes when it encounters something new. It acts as a civil engineer, creating new buildings and highways between different locations.

Understanding and taking this process to heart is the key to cultivating a growth mindset. To put it simply, when people believe that change is possible, they are more likely to feel positive about and embrace learning and growing.

Of course, embracing change can be scary. Growing and getting out of your comfort zone can make your heart pitter-patter. Here are a few reasons you might be staying within the safety of your comfort zones:

- **I do not have enough time.** The truth is that we make time for things that we prioritize and prioritize things that we consider important.

It may be too difficult to prioritize stress management, so I want you to prioritize your vision for your life. How much longer can you exist while feeling misaligned with your vision for your life? You will feel more satisfied and less stressed if your actions are in sync with your purpose and if you're able to strive for your goals without hesitation. Let that be the motivation to carve out time in your schedule to manage stress and work toward your life's vision.

- **I don't know where to start.** Congratulations! You have already started by picking up this book and reading a couple of chapters.

To keep up your progress, accountability is essential. It can be pivotal in staying on the right track and ultimately becoming successful. Here, I am not talking about an accountability partner but rather being held accountable by a coach or mentor who has your best interests at heart and will encourage you to be the best version of yourself. You are your most valuable asset, so investing time and money into your growth should not be a limiting factor.

- **I'm not capable or deserving.** These types of thoughts are known as limiting beliefs. They are false attitudes that you think are true.

Limiting beliefs often develop due to childhood experiences and may be triggered by many things we encounter in our adult lives. Limiting beliefs hold you back from even trying to reach your goals. You can overcome them with awareness, assessment, alignment, and affirmation.

You must first identify the limiting beliefs your mind holds onto. Next, assess rationally if the belief is true or not. Do you actually have objective examples to back up this belief, or are these thoughts founded on experiences that were colored by other factors? It may help to assess your limiting beliefs with the help of a loved one who can look at your situation with an unbiased perspective. This is followed by aligning your beliefs with the truth. Be honest with yourself about what your abilities really are. Finally, create an affirmation that will empower you to burst the cycle of your limiting beliefs.

For example, instead of believing that you're no good at public speaking, you can tell yourself that you haven't yet learned good speaking skills or haven't had the opportunity to practice these skills in helpful settings.

- **I don't know what I really want in life.** The last excuse for staying in your comfort zone is a lack of clarity on what you really want out of life or uncertainty about how you are going to achieve it.

Establishing your past story through step one of the SHAPE framework can help you get started, but you may still be stuck on where to go next. You need a clear understanding of who you are, and you can gain this knowledge through self-awareness.

Use Self-Awareness to Hone In On What You Want

You can't make effective decisions in your life unless you have a foundation of reality to work from. Self-awareness includes knowing your positive and negative triggers so that you can:

- **SHAPE more pleasant experiences to elicit positive emotions.** Think about how much time you spend engaged in activities or surrounded by people who align with your values. Strive to add more things you enjoy into your life, and a greater sense of happiness will follow.

This step may include pursuing simple things that you know bring you peace or laughter. Make the time to schedule more date nights with your partner. Carve out extra time each day to play with your children or catch up with friends.

Developing more self-awareness can also help you create more of these pleasant experiences.

For example, you may notice from your journaling that you tend to be in a better mood after engaging in a particular activity, such as baking or spending time in your garden. Is there a way to add more of this activity into your life? Can you take your hobby to the next level by making more time for it in your schedule, enrolling in a class, or connecting with others who also participate in this activity?

- **SHAPE the possibility of acting proactively instead of reactively.** This skill can allow you to respond more appropriately and intelligently.

When you're reactive, you respond to each little issue as it arises. You spend most of your time just trying to put out fires and dreading the next problem lurking around the corner. However, when you understand yourself better, you can become proactive. You can start to anticipate challenges and take steps to mitigate them or address them in advance. This is a very important part of living a more stress-free life.

- **SHAPE a habit of creating distance between you and your emotions.** Although it may feel like it at times, you are not your feelings or thoughts. You are a separate entity. You can let your emotions arise and then pass through you, keeping in mind that they are simply temporary states.

When you can look back and see what you have been through in the past, it's easier to remember that you have been here before. You have felt this sorrow, anger, or fear in the past and eventually moved on from it. You will move on from it again.

More self-awareness can help you view your situations more dispassionately and understand that your reaction to situations is something you do rather than something you are.

- **SHAPE your tools for positive change.** Think of your mistakes and misjudgments as stepping stones to improve yourself.

Self-awareness allows you to see your mistakes more clearly. If you have a fixed mindset, you may fall into the trap of believing that you are doomed to repeat these mistakes—or worse—time and time again. However, remembering that your brain is very adaptable and flexible can help you see that you can use your mistakes as learning experiences. What can you take away from a past mistake? Find something you can carry forward and use it to shape your future experiences.

- **SHAPE your presence so your mind is in the moment.** Less stress comes from being aware of what's around you and who you are at this exact point in time. Try to develop a habit of being grounded in the present moment rather than being lost in the past or constantly worrying about the future.

One great way to accomplish this is through grounding exercises. These activities connect you with the here and now. They can fight stress, help relieve symptoms of anxiety and depression, and boost your overall well-being.

For a simple grounding exercise, breathe in while counting to four, hold for four seconds, and exhale for four seconds. Repeat this exercise three times.

Notice what the air feels like as it enters and leaves your body. Place one hand on your chest and the other on your stomach and feel them expand. Try to pick up on as many sensations as you can.

Repeat this exercise when you notice signs of stress creeping in, or set an alarm on your phone and practice grounding yourself at a certain time each day.

Self-awareness is simply paying attention and increasing your understanding of yourself.

It is ultimately a habit applied over a long period of time — you can't check in with yourself once and think you have the full picture. Although it may take a decade or more to truly know yourself, you can make huge strides quickly! We are naturally oblivious to ourselves. Most of us don't have an accurate opinion of how the world views us. Knowing yourself will boost your ability to manage stress and enhance every aspect of your life.

However, it's not enough to simply notice and understand the triggers for your emotions or reactions to them. You need to do something with this information. You need to learn how to regulate yourself and develop self-control.

Practicing Self-Regulation

Self-regulation is a skill that you can use to respond to the things happening around you in a way that aligns with your vision of who you are and what you want for yourself. It's being intentional about your actions rather than reacting in a way that you later regret.

There are two types of self-regulation. Emotional self-regulation is the ability to control or influence your emotions. Behavioral self-regulation is the ability to make decisions and act in your long-term self-interest in accordance with your values.

Self-awareness is the foundation of self-regulation. You need to first understand where you are now, your motivations, and your values before you can practice acting out those values.

Like any other skill, self-regulation is something that you can learn and improve at.

Enhancing your ability to self-regulate is like learning how to assess a patient: it gets better with practice. This powerful skill can make your life better in countless ways and allow you to turn yourself into your greatest ally. I want to provide you with a few proven activities to help you start to practice self-regulation:

- **SHAPE time to meditate.** Meditation helps you to notice when your attention strays. This ability extends to noticing when your emotions are getting off-kilter, like a train unexpectedly jumping tracks. The ability to maintain a meditative state is great practice for bringing your emotions back in line, too.

There are many ways to meditate. The simplest form of meditation is simply to pay attention to your breathing. When your thoughts start to wander—and they will—bring them back to your breathing without judging your thoughts or thinking of them as "good" or "bad." You can also try many different resources to help with your practice. There are a wide variety of books and podcasts about meditation. If you want to listen to a guided meditation, in which someone walks you through what to do step-by-step, download a meditation app on your phone or search for free meditation videos on YouTube.

I want you to commit to meditating for five minutes, five days in a row, in five different locations. Each day, choose a new spot, such as your couch, office chair, or even the floor. Set a timer or cue up a guided exercise, and press start. Once you've completed your five days, check in with yourself and see what worked and what didn't. Which location worked best? Did you prefer to sit and breathe, or do you like using guided meditations? Build meditation into your daily practice, eventually increasing the amount of time you spend on this activity. See if you can work up to fifteen or even thirty minutes.

- **SHAPE your physical activity habits.** When your body is moving, your brain releases feel-good chemicals called endorphins that help minimize your body's stress response. Getting in the habit of being active is a great stress-busting tool and a way to regulate your reactions during stressful situations.

Does this mean you need to hit the gym for an intense workout every single day? Absolutely not! Being more active can be as simple as going on a walk a couple of times per week, doing some weekly gardening, or setting an alarm to take a break from work every afternoon and spend five minutes stretching. You can also use a fitness tracker or smartwatch to track your daily steps and gradually increase your step goals over time.

- **SHAPE your sleep schedule.** Research has shown that getting adequate sleep is essential for regulating your emotions. You're more susceptible to making poor decisions when you don't get enough sleep. You're also more likely to be impulsive and have less control over your emotions.

Using Self-Awareness To Find Your Purpose

As a part of the Stress Blueprint Academy, I have clients identify their life purpose so they can utilize it as motivation to work through their stressors. One of my clients, Nikhil, felt exceptionally stressed while working a high-pressure job, moving across the country, and caring for his mother, who was diagnosed with cancer. When I asked him to identify his purpose, he was stumped. This question challenged him because he had never thought about it before. He asked for more time to think about it.

This is a very common reaction to questioning your purpose. Many people do not think about why they exist, what the world needs, what they are good at, and what they can be paid for. And I'm not talking about monetary payment. I'm talking about identifying what lights you up to the point where you illuminate the path for others to find their way in this world.

Thinking about your purpose can be overwhelming, but that's not my intention here. If this question is too big or tough for you right now, you might want to explore your goals in life. What are you currently working toward in the personal, professional, financial, spiritual, emotional, or social aspects of your life?

Nikhil eventually figured out his purpose. He determined that he was a giver. He always wanted to help others and be there for his loved ones. However, in the process of doing this, he often put his own needs on the back burner. Nikhil's journey going through SHAPE showed him that his current purpose was to learn more about himself and put himself first. He realized he wasn't always meeting his own needs in his quest to pour himself out to others. Nikhil's new purpose in life was to look within and learn to feed himself.

I challenge you to revisit your purpose and your goals regularly. Honestly evaluate whether you are on track and whether these goals still make sense. If your job involves regularly developing goals or going through an evaluation, you may want to consider adding your life goals to this process so that your manager can help hold you accountable.

Questions for Reflection

Do you operate with a fixed mindset or a growth mindset?

Think back to a tough situation that you recently faced. What did your actions say about your mindset? Did you embrace the challenge as a learning experience, or did you back down when things got tough?

_____

_____

_____

_____

What excuses do you use to avoid growing and changing?

We all carry beliefs that force us to stay in our comfort zone. What thoughts and attitudes might be holding you back from trying something new?

_____

_____

_____

_____

What are your values, and do they align with your current routine?

Write down the things in life that are most important to you. What matters most? Now, reflect on whether you are living these values throughout your day-to-day life. Would your family and friends be surprised by the values you listed based on your words and actions?

_____

_____

_____

_____

How can you improve your self-awareness?

What strategies listed here resonate with you? What are some ways you can add more periods of reflection into your daily or weekly routine?

_____

_____

_____

_____

Activity:
Hone in On What You Want

Your next step is to focus on creating a life vision. Once you've crafted the story of all the past life events that make you you, think about your story's next chapter. Envision your ideal life. In this vision, where are you? What are you doing? What would it look like if your current stressors were eliminated or lessened? Write down what your vision includes in detail. Include the goals you'd like to achieve across multiple different aspects of life, including your professional, personal, family, social, and spiritual roles.

STEP 3: Assess

What tools do you need to reach your goals?

CHAPTER 5:

Loss of Control

"You have absolute control over but one thing, and
that is your thoughts."

—Napoleon Hill

Kelly was a client of mine who felt incredibly stressed out about her busy grad school schedule. She had a lot of major deadlines for school on her horizon, and as a result, her sleep schedule took a major hit. This left her constantly tired and feeling like she couldn't be at her best. She realized she needed to make a change before things got even more out of control, but didn't know where to start on her own.

Our conversations soon highlighted that one of the main causes of this stress was the feeling that she needed to be in control at all times. Everything in her schedule was very tightly regimented, causing her to panic when external factors required her to make changes.

I worked with Kelly on learning to give up control. We explored what could happen if she lost some of this need for organization. What would be the result if she didn't do everything in her schedule? What would it be like to focus on a few priorities and learn to let go of all those little stressful details that get in the way of the bigger picture?

Relinquishing some of that control—acknowledging that she didn't have to do everything and be everything for everybody—didn't come easily or naturally to Kelly. However, by investing in her self-care and working through the SHAPE framework, Kelly gained the tools she needed to succeed. She analyzed where stress was building up in her life, reevaluated her priorities, and learned new strategies to manage the different tasks she'd been juggling. She also says she learned a lot from others in the program dealing with their own stressors.

Ultimately, Kelly successfully got her degree, and she learned to live a life in which her stressors weren't affecting her ability to function and get things done.

Everyone can relate to wanting to be in charge. We become burdened by worries about things outside our control, we want to feel like we can fix things for the people we care about, and we desire to feel like we are "successful" by accomplishing specific goals.

But we don't actually have complete control over our lives. We are powerless over a lot of things. As unexpected as it may sound, letting go of control can bring a lot of beauty into your life. It's crucial to constantly appreciate that beauty because doing so makes relinquishing control easier.

To begin, giving up control requires far less work and energy than attempting to be in charge of everything. We stress and prepare for many things that we ultimately have no control over, meaning that a lot of this mental effort is wasted. Instead, we can save energy and use it where we have control, on the things that matter most, rather than exhausting it on external stressors.

Making decisions is much simpler when we relinquish control. It's challenging to predict the exact circumstances that will make us happy, understand what we need, and match what others expect of us. Yes, it's acceptable to have backup plans. However, I've discovered that managing my thoughts and energy to be flexible is preferable to trying to thoroughly prepare for every possible outcome.

When we become fixated on achieving a precise result, we become closed-minded and unreceptive to other possibilities. You can access all your options and ideas by letting go of the need to manage every little detail. You may even discover a transformative path you wouldn't have noticed if you stuck to your narrow perspective.

When we don't strive to control every aspect of our lives, we get to spend a lot more time being present, which is the only place we can truly live life.

How To Accept Loss of Control

The first step towards letting go of the need to control is realizing that you are not in charge. Life becomes a lot more bearable when you stop trying to control things that you can't. Be honest with yourself about what is and isn't within your power to change.

You can't control people, to start with. You have no power over their behavior, responses, thoughts, emotions, and beliefs. Additionally, you are NOT RESPONSIBLE for the way other people act, think, or feel. Once you accept that this isn't something you can change, you can let go of some of your desire to control the situation around you.

You also can't impact the nature of reality. For instance, you do not influence the weather, time, or death. Chance is uncontrollable. Additionally, you cannot make the world behave in the way you choose.

You must realize many aspects of yourself are beyond your control. You have no control over what your body requires regarding food, water, sleep, and other essentials. Emotions are also something you cannot completely control. Sorry. You are unable to change the biological and early-life predispositions you have.

And finally, no matter how diligently you plan and work, you will never fully have power over how any scenario will turn out. There are just too many variables involved for you to have any kind of control.

Responding to a Loss of Control

Just because there are many things that you can't directly influence doesn't mean you're powerless. You generally have control over your behaviors and responses. When your life seems out of control, keep your attention on your current actions and thoughts to maintain perspective. For example, while you don't always have control over your emotions, you can learn to let them go rather than clinging to them.

The things you have control over must be found internally, not externally. Depending on how much energy you have, some of these things might not seem like they are within your reach. You can, nevertheless, get a little better at dealing with loss of control with experience and practice. Try the following strategies:

- **Make a list of what you can and can't control.** When dealing with a situation in which you feel powerless, making a list is a great method for visualizing your options. Worriers or overthinkers will benefit the most from this activity.

Think carefully about all the elements around you. Which external elements are determined by other factors? Which elements are primarily internal and, therefore, affected by your response? In other words, who is pulling the puppet strings? Try to be honest with yourself when it comes to which things you can and can't affect.

- **Keep your plans open.** There's nothing wrong with being prepared. However, planning for every possible outcome is impossible, especially when finances, deadlines, or other individuals are involved.

Try to plan for the things that truly need to be thought out in advance. You can consider tiny details but avoid writing them down in black and white. When you prepare things ahead of time and then need to re-plan later, you will waste a lot of time and energy. Being flexible, on the other hand, can help you save your efforts and keep you open to opportunities. Additionally, you'll spare yourself from disappointment if things don't turn out as anticipated.

- **Don't be too invested in the result.** Along with being adaptable in your objectives, you should work on not being emotionally invested in particular results.

Should we "hope for the best" or "expect the worst" in both life and death? What if, instead, we committed to being in the truth of whatever is present and practiced cultivating non-judgmental attention?

Keep in mind that numerous variables can affect an outcome, and we cannot control them all. There is no way to know with certainty what will happen. Be open to possible outcomes but avoid becoming emotionally invested in them because they cannot be guaranteed.

- **Embrace change, or at least accept it.** The fact that things always change is a fact of life. You must be open to this idea before you can relinquish control.

I encourage you to go one step further in this process by learning to embrace change. I do this by realizing that change offers the best chance for personal development as well as the discovery of novel and interesting things. What are the advantages of change? How do you show appreciation for change?

- **Strive for personal development.** Instead of attempting to alter your situation, focus on personal development.

We change as a result of being forced to confront the fact that we can no longer control every aspect of our lives. You may learn to let go of worries, slow down, set priorities, and concentrate on the things that mean most to you rather than trying to change the unchangeable.

Spend some time dealing with the issues preventing you from letting go of control, and then concentrate on your progress in that area.

- **Be there.** Be present, above all else. There is no point in lingering on the past because we cannot change what has occurred. We also have no influence over what will occur in the future.

When you pause to think about being present, it's a very lovely thing. Even during sad or difficult periods, when I reflect on all the times I was genuinely there, everything was okay at that time. I can let go of control when I remind myself that life seems as it should when I stay in the now, even if the future moments aren't exactly planned.

Learning to let go and choosing to focus your energy on the things within your power can be very freeing. It is an important part of discovering your life purpose and determining what you need to take the next steps forward.

CHAPTER 6

Assess Your Toolbox

"You have the power to change perception, to inspire and empower, to show people how to embrace their complications and flaws and see the true beauty that's inside all of us."

—Beyonce

So far, you've worked on telling your life story and honing in on your vision for your future life. The next step is to assess. You are now in the beginning stages of getting from where you are to where you want to be. During this part of the SHAPE framework, you will introspectively survey what you currently have in your toolbelt and what you need to add. You likely already have some of the skills, beliefs, or experiences that will help you manifest your vision. These factors may have helped you successfully move beyond stressful situations in the past. However, there are also some tools that you probably need to learn or develop.

Before embarking on this next step, we will take some time to learn about resilience's ability to combat stress.

The Power of Resilience

As we learned in Chapter 1, stress occurs when our minds and bodies are put under strain because they are forced to adapt to some sort of new change or stressor.

Resilience is the other side of this coin. It is the ability to bounce back from adversity and continue moving forward when stressed. It is staying strong, being willing to change, and transforming yourself to meet the demands of your stressors. It can be incredibly difficult to remain resilient, but it can also help you grow in ways that wouldn't otherwise be possible.

I was able to exemplify resilience when one decision changed my vision for my life. I remember standing in the kitchen one day, leaning with my back pressed against the kitchen counter, my arms folded across my chest, and my legs crossed at the ankle.

I was deep in thought, reflecting on the caregiving burden that I had seen placed on so many of my cancer patients over the years. However, this was not just a professional matter but also a personal one. I had been watching my aunt's transition from sister to caregiver in the wake of another aunt's diagnosis of glioblastoma, a type of brain tumor. As a cancer patient, my aunt required a lot of support from the time of diagnosis through surgeries to hospice and, eventually, death. My other aunts had stepped up to fill gaps in care despite not having any medical knowledge, but I could see that they needed support, too, and I wanted to take action to help other families in similar situations.

My husband entered the kitchen, stood right before me, and asked, "What's wrong? What are you thinking about?"

I looked up and stared at him for a few seconds before asking, "Should I start that organization for cancer caregivers?"

Without hesitating or even a blink of the eyes, he replied, "Yes. Why not?"

In my mind, I was contemplating why I shouldn't pursue this dream. We were in the middle of a pandemic. We had a new baby. I had just committed to returning to the front lines and caring for patients. Instead, the words poured out of my mouth: "Great! What should we call it?"

We spent the next few minutes going back and forth on names before it hit me. "SHAPE Partners! We are shaping partnerships to provide optimal impact."

"What does SHAPE stand for?" my husband asked.

I immediately had my answer ready. "Sunflower because I love sunflowers, Health Advocacy as we want cancer caregivers to be champions for their loved ones' health, and

Personal Empowerment so that we can empower caregivers to care for themselves."

My husband looked at me with his hand on his chin. "I like it," he responded. And just like that, the next step of my vision was born.

My mission with SHAPE Partners was to help cancer caregivers optimize their mental and physical health by managing their stress. This would allow them to better advocate for themselves and their loved ones. I hoped that both those with cancer and those who cared for them could create a better vision for themselves and learn how to practice self-care more effectively.

Even though I had no business experience and my mind contained many doubts and worries, I forged forward. The first thing I did was create time to strategize ways to get my service into the hands of cancer caregivers. The first stop: social media. I made a Facebook page and started posting content. Eventually, I wanted to provide more, so I began "going live" on Facebook without any prior experience.

When it came time for my first live video, I was sweating bullets as I set everything up, trying to get the height of the laptop right and the lighting in the optimal position. I hit the "Go Live" button, and then ... nothing. I stared into the camera, saying, "Am I live? I am not sure. I think I am live. Will I see a record button?" I later found out I was recording live the entire time! It was quite the experience, but I was focused on the mission of service. After this first successful attempt, I scheduled live videos weekly and called the segment "Wednesdays with Wendy." Cancer caregivers, friends, and family members quickly began attending and said they found my videos helpful. By staying resilient in the face of doubts and mistakes, I was able to bring value into the world.

We sometimes have brilliant ideas that we keep mulling over in our heads. It's tempting to allow the desire for planning and perfection to take over, keeping the ideas stuck in a place where they do not provide value.

However, the time we waste mulling over ideas is time we steal from someone in the world to share in the value we can create. People are waiting for that idea to be birthed and shared with the world. Someone is waiting on your gift to help move them forward in their own life's vision.

At this moment, you may feel like you're not completely ready to take action. You need to wait until you're "ready." Remember that small steps may be good enough to share with others to enrich their lives! Your 40% can be the exact percentage someone else needs to add to their 60% to bring them 100% to their vision.

It is essential to take imperfect action. Consider looking at the impact you can have if you take one step towards aligning or executing your purpose. What would that look and feel like?

Building Resilience
Through the Six Domains

Experts have identified six domains of resilience. Each domain is a different skill or behavior that can help make a person more resilient. The domains are tools that you can add to your toolbox to help you get where you want to go. These areas are important and help determine how you respond to negative experiences. Likewise, improving each domain can help you learn to better manage stress. The six domains are:

- **Vision.** Vision includes reflecting upon your purpose and your goals. Both can serve as anchors and sources of motivation on your stress management journey.

Your goals are stepping stones to your purpose. They describe how you aim to share your gifts with the world. Your purpose is that intangible "thing" that internally lights you up and spreads your light to others, touching them in ways they did not even know needed to be touched. Your purpose is how you can transform the world, one person at a time.

Fully understanding your vision can help you be more decisive and illuminate the next steps you need to take. It helps align your attitudes and actions toward one clear path. Additionally, by encouraging you to keep the big picture in mind, vision can give you perspective and allow you to view minor challenges as stepping stones to get to where you want to be.

- **Health.** When you are free from disease or illness, whether physical or mental, you can be your best self.

This domain explores your personal wellness foundation, which includes physical activity, good nutrition, and adequate sleep. This trifecta solidifies the most important factor on this journey: YOU! When you fulfill the health domain, you can see your vision more clearly, and it becomes easier to overcome your stressors.

- **Composure.** Your vision helps dictate your composure, or awareness and regulation of your emotions.

It's natural to suddenly face intense emotions when dealing with a stressor, and these feelings aren't always things you can directly control. However, you can choose whether you give in to your negative instincts or respond to them in a more positive, healthy manner. Stepping back from a stressful situation, calming yourself, and proactively preparing yourself to respond can help you maintain your composure.

If you are in tune with your emotions and work toward building emotional intelligence, you can better resist relinquishing your power to external stressors. You can then transfer that power back into yourself to serve your purpose.

- **Reasoning.** Giving that power back to yourself requires the reasoning domain, which includes critical thinking and problem-solving skills.

This domain requires composure. When you're able to keep your emotions in check, you can more clearly exhibit reasoning by thinking through challenges and planning your next move in a rational way rather than a reactive one.

This domain also includes planning ahead. When you have more self-awareness, you can anticipate or predict that certain challenges may arise or that you may be tempted to react a particular way in a given situation. Reasoning helps you develop a clear plan while taking into account potential pitfalls.

- **Collaboration.** This domain represents social wellness, highlighting the importance of having or building a supportive network to empower you to stay on track with what is important: your purpose.

Your vision for yourself most likely can't be accomplished on your own. Establishing meaningful connections with others, working together, receiving, and giving support can help you reach your goals and improve in all of the other domains of resilience.

- **Tenacity.** This domain refers to persistence or grit. It results in the bounce back, or what I like to call the bounce forward.

Tenacity is about continuing to work hard over time rather than bailing when facing a problem. It involves being realistic about the fact that you will face struggles but not allowing those struggles to overcome your vision. If you've ever been called stubborn, that trait may help you here!

Improving in these domains can help you uncover more of your gifts and talents. By learning to stay the course, you may find that your vision and goals change and lead you to unexpected places.

SHAPE Partners led me to become a certified life coach, speaker, and trainer. These roles weren't something I had in mind when I first set foot on campus at Saint Joseph College. Instead, they were the natural result of understanding myself better and honing a vision of what I wanted.

Assessing Your Abilities

Research shows that prolonged stress can reduce the gray matter in your brain. This impacts your memory, emotions, and even thinking. Therefore, one of the first things I have SHAPE clients do is create the GAP—the Gray Area to Pause, Process, Purpose, Pivot, and Proceed. This helps people assess what is in their toolbox and discover what we need to add to align with our vision. How do we operate in the GAP? There are a few key steps:

1. **Pause.** First, review your schedule and block off five minutes a day for five days. Carve out time to stop and be with your own thoughts. Each day, ensure you set your alarm as a reminder for your five minutes of GAP time. At the start of GAP time, pause with intention. Stop everything you are doing. Then, take five deep breaths. This helps reset your mind and direct your attention to the current moment.

2. **Process.** Next, focus on your current perspective to gain insight into the current stressors in your life. De-

termine if they are internal or external and examine how much control you have over each one.

3. **Purpose.** Consider whether your stressors are aligning or misaligning with your purpose or goals. Look at the things on your calendar or analyze your daily habits — do they align with your vision?

4. **Pivot.** Use this information to consider whether you need to reset your GPS or whether you need to plan to go in a different direction that aligns with your purpose. Do you have to change your mindset or reframe your thoughts around these stressors? Decide how to best manage these stressors. How many of these stressors are within your control? If you have control over some aspects, you can rationally think through how to address them. If they are not within your power to change, work on releasing yourself from worrying about them. This is easier said than done, but with practice, it does become easier.

5. **Proceed.** After you process these questions and answers, you can implement your plan to get mentally unstuck from your stressors. Now is the time when you decide if you need to keep pursuing your current route because you have a clear path or pivot and change direction to get back on track with your purpose or goals. Finally, before breaking this GAP cycle, take five deep breaths.

The GAP process allowed me to assess what I had and what I needed to start and amplify SHAPE Partners. Between breastfeeding, completing paperwork to start a new job, and keeping my family safe from COVID-19, I had to pause and mentally compartmentalize. I thought about the external stressors of the world and carefully considered my purpose in life to serve the cancer-caregiver population. I determined that I had to pivot my focus to reach my audience and start to serve.

This process also included assessing my toolbelt and determining what I needed. I had a lot of experience dealing with cancer patients and their caregivers, giving me a lot of knowledge surrounding the issues that caregivers faced. I also already knew how to access and use social media to reach more people. However, I didn't have all of the knowledge and skills I needed to start a company and maintain a business. Instead of letting these things stop me, I took action. I hired a business coach to help show me the way and teach me how to sustain this new organization.

This eventually resulted in another amazing business, The Stress Blueprint, being born. In this new endeavor, I aimed to empower healthcare leaders, nurses, and student nurses to optimize their personal and professional development through stress management and emotional intelligence (EQ) using our signature SHAPE framework.

Carving Out Time for Yourself

Psychoanalysts have found that emotional maturity is the ability to spend time alone without any television, computers, or smartphones. It is amazing the joy that can come from being alone. It can help you think more deeply about the stressors in your life. And when you're emotionally and mentally prepared, you'll be better able to meet them head-on. Being in your own company allows you to see where you are and what you need to get where you want to be.

When you're constantly in the company of others, there's pressure on you to conform. For instance, it's difficult for people to eat a healthy diet and work out when they are surrounded by friends and family members who abstain from these behaviors. The next time you are around like-minded people, observe yourself objectively and compare your observations when you are around people who are more different from you. You may find that you behave differently. Therefore, when working through the SHAPE framework and assessing different aspects of your life, schedule adequate alone time to minimize other influences.

If you spend at least half an hour each day looking back at the previous day and analyzing how you lived it, you'll gain some great insights. It's an empowering feeling to uncover the gems in your toolbox and discover the unexpected resources in your life. They can help you face the existing gaps that require fulfillment to align with your purpose. That's the power of perspective.

WENDY GARVIN MAYO · 115

What is your vision for your life? The answer to this question is critical. The GAP is a tool required to transform your unfavorable stress management solutions—or lack thereof—as well as bad habits and a negative mindset. The process begins only when you can pinpoint the stressors in your life. The next step is to think deeply about how the stressors have affected the physical, social, spiritual, occupational, and emotional aspects of your life. The final step is to desire change and create a plan.

Questions for Reflection

Where do you stand with each of the six domains of resilience?

Vision — What goals are you currently working toward in your life?

_____

_____

Health — On a scale of 1 to 5, with 1 being "not good" and 5 being "exceptional," how are you doing at meeting your needs for physical activity, nutrition, and sleep?

_____

_____

Composure — When faced with an unexpected problem, do you tend to respond calmly or react in anger?

_____

_____

Reasoning — How often do you take time to pause and consider how to respond to current challenges or potential future issues?

_____

_____

Collaboration — What is your support network like? Who can you count on to be there for you during stressful times and successes?

_____

_____

Tenacity — Think back to a long-term problem that you faced. Did you continue to put in work to address the issue, or did you step away?

_____

_____

How can you take the time for yourself that you need?

Develop a plan to give yourself more time to reflect regularly. What time of day is your mind most willing to tackle challenges? Where is a place where you can get some uninterrupted alone time to assess and plan?

_____

_____

_____

_____

Activity:
Assess What You Have and What You Need

Think about your purpose and goals. Make a list of what you need to get there from where you currently stand. Which items do you currently have in your toolbelt? Think of possible experiences, attitudes, beliefs, habits, skills, or knowledge that you already have that may help serve you. Now consider the GAP. What do you still need to complete your vision? Write down some ideas of how you can obtain that experience, knowledge, or skill.

STEP 4: Plan

*What are the next steps you need to take that
can help you get to where you want to be?*

CHAPTER 7:

The Six Stages
of Behavior Change

"If you are going to achieve excellence in big things,
you develop the habit in little matters. Excellence is
not an exception,
it is a prevailing attitude."

—Colin Powell

Studies have revealed that changing behavior is actually a more intricate and circular process. The stages of change model, sometimes referred to as the trans-theoretical model of change, is a well-recognized method developed by experts to describe a person's motivation levels when modifying their behavior.

A change typically doesn't occur all at once, according to this model. Instead, it is a process. It starts with being aware of behavior you don't like, continues when you manage to get rid of the old behavior, and ends when you successfully create a new habit that better serves you.

James Prochaska, one of the researchers who developed this model, established six stages of behavior change while researching smokers who were able to successfully quit. Regardless of what changes you hope to make, you can successfully modify your actions if you know these six stages.

1. Precontemplation

"Precontemplation" is a term used to describe the time before you become aware that a change is needed. In other words, precontemplation is denial.

When you are in the precontemplation stage, you are experiencing a problem, but you won't admit that something needs to change. Even when everyone around you might be able to see that things aren't going well, you maintain that the matter is not too serious for you to handle or that someone else is to blame. You may not even realize that changing your behavior or building a new habit could greatly impact your stress levels. You're like an ostrich with its head buried in the sand.

To progress to the next step, you need to accept that a change may be needed. Change won't happen until you decide that the price of upholding the problematic habit is higher than the price of change.

Completing the previous steps of the SHAPE framework—telling your story, honing in on your vision, and assessing your toolset—will set you up to move past the precontemplation stage. These actions will provide more self-awareness and help you better understand what in your life needs a change.

For example, in this stage, an individual may not be aware that their stress levels are a problem, or they may not recognize the need for change. They may deny or minimize the impact of stress on your life. They may think their stress is just a normal and unavoidable part of life.

2. Contemplation

Once you move past the precontemplation stage, you are ready to accept the reality of the problem. You realize that you are dealing with stressors and start to understand how they impact various aspects of your life, including your mental and physical health. You are prepared to weigh your options. The learning phase of contemplation is when you gather information.

During this stage, you weigh the advantages and disadvantages of the options open to you. You may also consider the benefits and drawbacks of changing how things are done. This is a stage in which you start to gather knowledge but have yet to take any action.

You may bounce back and forth between the precontemplation and contemplation stages before you feel ready to proceed. When you accept the need for change in light of your analysis, you are prepared to advance to the next level.

For example, at this stage, individuals begin to recognize that their stress is affecting their well-being and consider making a change. They may start thinking about the pros and cons of reducing stress and its potential benefits. The individual might acknowledge that their stress negatively impacts their sleep, relationships, and overall quality of life.

3. Planning

The next stage is to determine how to carry out your decision to make a change in your life. You prepare to alter your behavior. What are the steps that you can take to see your vision realized?

During the planning stage, you specify your objective. You study possible approaches to achieving your goals. Here, you may start to look for outside guidance. For example, when stressors are taking over your life, a stress management program or coach can empower you to effectively manage your stress by helping you develop sustainable habits. A life coach or mentor can teach you about what you need and help guide your path.

You are prepared to take action once you have created a viable plan. For example, in the planning stage, individuals actively start planning to take action to reduce their stress. They may seek information, explore different strategies, and set goals. They may research stress management techniques, sign up for a yoga class or the Stress Blueprint Academy, or start practicing relaxation exercises.

4. Action

During the action phase, you carry out your plan. This stage can be thought of as an experiment in which you discover which elements of your strategy work and where the unanticipated challenges are.

The process of changing behavior inevitably involves switching back and forth between planning and action. No strategy is perfect, and you'll probably need to return to the drawing board several times. It's critical to see any issues as a chance to enhance your plan.

You may reach this stage after you have found a program like The Stress Blueprint and you start working with a coach to explore stressors, create your vision, examine your toolbox, and create an action plan.

For example, in the action stage, individuals actively modify their behavior and adopt specific stress management techniques or coping mechanisms. They put their plans into practice and make a conscious effort to reduce their stress levels. They might start incorporating daily meditation, SHAPE framework, or exercise routines into their schedule to manage stress.

5. Maintenance

Once your action plan is running smoothly, you are prepared to enter the most difficult stage of all: maintenance.

This stage of behavior change is where you keep up your good work. You actively and intentionally work to stay on track to prevent relapse.

Most people are excited and energized when they first enter the action stage. As you start to see positive change and enjoy this transformation's advantages, you may experience a sense of exhilaration.

The task of maintaining your new habit over time is significantly harder. When you get farther away from your old behavior, you may forget the pain it caused. Some temptations can be challenging to reject.

During this stage, it's essential to have ongoing support from others. Look to communities, peers, loved ones, and mentors to propel you forward and avoid slipping back into old habits.

There are usually lapses during the maintenance period. This is all okay and part of the learning process. To correct these errors, it might be necessary to go back to the planning or even contemplation stages. You may want to assess what worked for you or analyze what caused you to go back to previous behaviors.

Some people who fall off the wagon during the maintenance stage become so discouraged that they return to the precontemplation stage. Don't allow this to happen to you! Understanding that behavior change rarely happens in a straight line enables you to swiftly get back on track after experiencing a setback.

For example, in this stage, the individual works to sustain the new behavior and prevent relapses. They continue to practice stress management techniques and actively manage their stress levels to ensure long-term well-being. They may consistently engage in activities that help them relax and manage stress, such as maintaining a regular exercise routine, practicing mindfulness, or seeking social support.

6. Relapse

If you're like most people, you'll relapse on the route to permanently quitting a habit or going through a behavior change.

Discouragement and a sense of failure are frequent companions to relapse.

Although relapsing can be upsetting, most people who successfully change their behavior do not take a direct route to a lifetime free of detrimental bad habits. Instead, they repeatedly cycle through the five stages before finally making a stable lifestyle adjustment.

As you try to build up or break down new habits, remember that relapses are common and aren't a sign that you should give up. When you return to doing something you want to quit, you might feel like a failure. Your self-confidence may take a big hit. However, rather than focusing on the failure, you can learn to consider how the slip occurred and view the situation as an opportunity to discover new coping mechanisms. Relapses can provide crucial chances for growth and learning.

Relapsing is like falling off a horse. The best next step is to get back on. It's important to avoid going all the way back to the precontemplation stage if you do take a fall. Instead, try to restart the process in the stages of planning, action, or even maintenance if you can.

People who have relapsed may need to consider additional changes. It might help you learn how to predict when you're at risk of slipping back into your old lifestyle or show you that you need to develop better coping mechanisms for stress. This could help you maintain more self-control as a result.

For example, during this relapse, the individual may struggle to prioritize self-care and stress management practices. They might start neglecting their meditation sessions, skipping workouts, and working longer hours without breaks. As a result, their stress levels begin to increase again, and they notice a decline in their overall well-being.

You can accomplish your objectives by being aware of the six behavior change stages and building support, accountability, and community. Once you are familiar with the patterns typical of the behavior change process, you will be equipped to handle any setbacks and resume your goals quickly.

CHAPTER 8

Make a Plan

"Be passionate and move forward with gusto every single hour of every single day until you reach your goal."

—Ava DuVernay

I first learned the importance of creating and carrying out a Plan the first time I changed careers. Although I was initially a Registered Nurse, I was certain that I was going back to school to obtain my master's degree as an Advanced Practice Registered Nurse (APRN). My dream job was to work as an outpatient oncology APRN. In other words, I wanted to specialize in caring for those living with cancer.

In 2010, this dream was realized. I graduated and got an APRN job. In April 2015, I sat in my windowless corner office with white walls and dated wall art. I was in the middle of charting—updating patient medical records—when it suddenly hit me. I stopped writing, looked up, and said to myself, "You made it." I was actually working my dream job and was so happy. I was the person who came into the office early when it was still quiet. I loved flooding the office with positive energy by greeting everyone with a big smile and a "good morning" as I walked through the halls. I was so in my element.

Not long after this incident, Don, a pharmaceutical sales representative, came by one day. He was well-known in our office for allowing us to order individual meals for his lunch and learn sessions. On this day, he came into my office and commented, "You would make a great Medical Science Liaison."

This was the first I had heard of this job. What was an MSL? I responded, "I am working my dream job, so I'm not interested in another position." Each time he came to the office after that, he ensured we discussed the MSL role. Then, one day, as I was sitting in my little corner office, I looked up, and Don was standing in my doorway with a huge smile on his face. I invited him into my office to have a seat. He smiled and said, "There's an MSL position open here in Connecticut, and I want to refer you."

"Thank you so much," I responded. "I will think about it."

Don continued, "I will put in the referral, and you can apply when you're ready. You will be perfect for the position, and we can work together." As he stood up and left my office, I felt a sense of pressure, even though nothing had happened yet. My emotions were getting the best of me.

Later that day, I went home, sat on the couch with my laptop, opened Google, and typed, "What is a Medical Science Liaison?" Suddenly, BOOM! My mood shifted as I read, "...medical science liaisons usually are doctorate prepared, holding a Ph.D. or PharmD." I figured I might as well apply—after all, Don had put in the referral—but I didn't think there was any chance they were going to hire me. After all, I was an APRN and didn't have a doctorate degree.

The Things That Hold You Back

We often create what I call less I do (LID) excuses for ourselves. These excuses include anything that holds you back from your full potential, seeing the possibilities, or finding your purpose. Your LID is that small voice in your head that has you saying, *I can't or I won't or I'll never*. Your LID holds you down and keeps you stagnant, preventing you from moving up. Once you remove your LID, the sky's the limit.

You tend to develop your LID over time, starting in your childhood years. It may take some time to decipher the little things your internal voice is telling you and figure out how it's been impacting your actions.

This internal mindset keeps us from living as our true selves and fully showing up in our greatness. My LID included my limiting beliefs that made me believe I didn't have a chance at getting this new position. Yes, I did apply, but I had already counted myself out, which may have impacted the way I completed the application or the way I showed up to the interview.

How do LID excuses show up in your life? Is it mind traps, negative self-talk, self-doubt, or procrastination? Identifying the LID mindset is essential as it prevents you from fully exploring possibilities, goals, or opportunities and creating a comprehensive plan. Living life without a plan is like driving aimlessly across the country without a map or GPS. A plan keeps you on track. Furthermore, when your plan is developed, visible, and utilized, it provides some level of self-accountability.

In May 2015, on a warm morning, I just finished seeing my last patient as I sat down at my desk and heard my cell phone ring. *Who would be calling me during work hours?* I picked up the phone and saw a Pennsylvania area code. I cautiously answered, "Hello?"

The voice on the other end excitedly said, "Good morning! My name is Sandy from Human Resources. May I speak with Wendy Garvin?"

"This is she. How can I help you?"

The words that came next made me drop the phone. "We want to offer you the MSL position!"

I felt like my mouth was hanging open as I sat at my desk. Feelings of stress immediately flooded back in. I finally mustered up the courage to say, "Thank you so much! Can I think about it and get back to you?"

"Sure thing," came the response.

After hanging up the phone, I started to cry. Unfortunately, they weren't happy tears. All I could think was, *What did you do?* I was working my dream job, and now I had to decide whether I should leave. It was a tough day.

The next day, I informed my attending physician about the call, and he said, "We don't want to lose you." My first thought was, *I don't want to leave either!*

As we were talking, another physician walked by, and my attending physician invited him into the conversation. The second physician commented, "You can always come back to clinical work, but you may not always have this opportunity."

Those words hit me hard. *I have to take this MSL position,* I thought. The words of John Maxwell rang true for me then: "If you are growing, you are always out of your comfort zone."

The next day, I reluctantly called Sandy and accepted the offer. I was nervous and scared about this opportunity because I never envisioned leaving my dream job and working in the pharmaceutical industry where I had no patient interaction. To limit my feelings of stress surrounding the situation, I decided to craft a plan: I would accept the job, give it three months, and then re-evaluate whether I wanted to continue or return to clinical practice.

In retrospect, I have to be totally honest and share that leaving clinical practice to enter the corporate world of pharmaceuticals was one of the best decisions I ever made. I was able to develop new abilities, such as innovative thinking, intellectual agility, and creativity. I even got the chance to hone my leadership skills. My experience in the corporate world has enhanced my ability to serve the nursing career on another level. My plan and willingness to try something new served me well.

Developing Good Habits

Let's do a quick exercise. You will need a piece of paper and a pen. First, make a list of your bad habits. Your bad habits are obstacles that stand in the way of creating the good habits you want to implement. For example, you may want to wake up earlier to start the day, but instead, you stay awake to watch the OWN network until three a.m.

Second, create positive alternatives that you can work toward. For example, you may write down, *I will go to bed at nine p.m. each night and DVR any shows I might want to watch later.* The key here is to replace the bad habit with a new habit that provides the same benefit. Giving up something pleasurable is very challenging, but finding an enjoyable substitute that doesn't feel like a sacrifice can help.

Lastly, review your list and move on to developing good habits.

Deciding to adopt new habits to manage stress can be difficult, especially if living a stressful life feels "normal" to you. You may be so used to feeling this way that it feels like you're doing something wrong when you don't have stressors breathing down your neck!

I want to provide you with a few strategies that can make developing new stress management habits easier:

- **Schedule your habits.** As soon as you decide to adopt a new habit, choose when it's going to get done and put it on your calendar. If it's not on the calendar, it's more likely not to get done.

For example, if you plan to start getting to sleep at nine p.m., set an alarm to start winding down and getting ready for bed at eight p.m. Having a specific time to perfect your new habits is instrumental in ensuring the habit becomes a regular part of your life.

- **Go slow.** Start with one habit at a time to increase your chances of success. It's natural to resist change, but remember that there are multiple stages that you have to go through when you're trying to adjust your behavior. Focusing on one thing at a time may help.

Once you're performing one habit reliably, add in another. Continue this until you've incorporated all the habits that you believe will relieve your stress and promote joy in your life.

There is also another benefit to building habits slowly rather than trying to change everything all at once. Willpower is only available in finite quantities. Adding multiple new habits simultaneously requires far more willpower than most of us have in reserve. There's no hurry when implementing good habits, so take whatever time is necessary to install each new habit completely before moving on to a new goal. It can take a month or even longer, so give yourself grace.

- **Do the easiest thing first.** Choose the behavior change that you believe will be the easiest to perform religiously. This will help set you up for success. One victory will encourage you to continue adding more positive habits and make your progress much smoother.

- **Answer the "why."** As you consider a new behavior you'd like to implement, consider what it will add to your life. If you're unable to clearly define the advantage of sticking with a particular habit, you'll be less likely to stay on track. Your "why" is your source of motivation.

- **Don't forget rewards.** Give yourself some pats on the back along the way. Even a single week of 100% compliance is a reason to celebrate! Keep the rewards small so you can have more of them.

You can also implement BOOM moments. When you stick to your plan of implementing your goals to create a new habit, verbally and physically yell out *BOOM!* Your brain will soon come to associate *BOOM* moments with success.

- **Be realistic.** Remember that progress will come slowly. Try to focus on each habit for thirty days, since psychologists often claim that it takes at least this long to create a new habit.

The first few days of behavior change might be easy, especially since you're most likely excited about your new goal and looking forward to where it can take you. But after a few days or a week, it may be harder to stick with your plan. That's where resilience comes in. Just remember, like other skills, creating new habits becomes easier the more you practice and work at it! Do everything you can to get through those first thirty days successfully. You'll likely keep the habit forever if you can survive that month. Stick with it! And remember, missing a single day here and there isn't a big deal. However, missing two consecutive days simply creates the habit of not doing the activity. In other words, if you miss one day, it's even more important to do your habit again the next day.

- **Define a trigger.** Habits work best when you have a trigger—something that reminds you to do them.

A good trigger is something that automatically happens each day or a habit you've already successfully developed. Your trigger for a particular habit could be getting out of bed, brushing your teeth, showering, putting on your shoes, eating lunch, driving to work, or sitting at your desk. Anything that you already do every day can serve as a reminder to perform your new habit. Get used to doing your new habit during or immediately after your established daily activity of choice.

- **Proactively prepare.** Some habits require planning, equipment, software, or other tools. If you're going to exercise in the morning, for example, you'll probably need to set your alarm to wake up earlier. It might also make sense to have your workout clothes laid out and ready to go.

Plan ahead and implement the necessary preparations to ensure your success. New habits can be challenging to develop, but these strategies will make it go more smoothly, especially if you use your available resources to help change your behavior.

Avoiding Pitfalls When Creating New Habits

Several things can go wrong when you try to develop a new routine. For one thing, relapse is bound to happen. There will be days when you skip right over your new habit. Therefore, it is important to have a contingency plan. For example, if you normally go on a run right after work, have a backup plan in case it's raining, or you have to work late. You could instead head to the gym, choose an indoor exercise you can perform at home, or go on a walk after dinner. Proactively choose a backup plan and have it ready to go *before* you need it.

Just as you can have things that remind you to complete your new habit, you can also experience factors that make it harder to perform that action. List your negative triggers—anything that distracts you from your new behaviors. For example, a particular friend who focuses on negative topics might get in the way of trying to cultivate a more positive mindset for yourself. Perhaps keeping the television on before bedtime leads to watching a movie until the early hours of the next morning. Being aware of these negative triggers can help you avoid them in the future, setting you up for success.

Take care to manage your expectations. Expecting too much too soon can have negative consequences. If you think you will immediately change your entire life overnight, you probably won't make it very far, and your failure to build new habits may be a source of negative self-talk in the future. However, it isn't necessary to be perfect. A few slip-ups aren't a reason to get upset and discard your new routine. Expect to experience challenges. Expect to sometimes miss the mark. Avoid putting too much pressure on yourself.

If you do slip up, you may be trying to do too much. Giving a task too much emphasis can make it appear less appealing. I recommend starting over even smaller. If you're consistently struggling, start over at the beginning, but this time, make it easier on yourself. Maybe thirty minutes of exercise is too overwhelming at the beginning. Start with one minute, even though one minute of exercise doesn't have a lot of practical value. It won't transform your health, but it will make getting two minutes of exercise a little easier next week. Taking small steps and making adjustments can ensure your long-term success.

Making a SMART Plan

All of these tips and tricks for creating good habits and avoiding pitfalls can be summarized by following the acronym SMART. A plan that follows these guidelines is most likely to be successful in helping you manage stress and transform your life. Make sure that your blueprint for action is:

- **Specific.** Set goals that are clearly defined and outlined. Your plan should paint a clear picture of exactly what you want the outcome to be.

When outlining a specific goal, write down exactly what you want to accomplish, the steps you will take, and what you will get out of the plan.

For example, saying that your goal is to "take better care of yourself" isn't precise. To make your plan specific, you could say, "Wake up thirty minutes earlier every morning to meditate and eat a healthy breakfast."

- **Measurable.** How will you know when your goal is complete or when your plan is finished? You need to decide how you will measure your progress.

Let's say that you need to learn a new skill to carry out your vision. "Learn how to use social media" isn't a measurable goal. How do you know when you're done? How do you know whether you've learned enough? Instead, your goal could be, "Take a social media class, set up an account on Facebook, and gain fifty followers."

- **Achievable.** This point is all about ensuring you are being reasonable and realistic with your expectations. Lasting change often happens slowly.

You can make sure your goals are achievable with the assess step in the SHAPE framework. Think about whether you have the tools you need or how you could gain new skills or knowledge.

To showcase this step, we can go back to my experience in creating SHAPE Partners. I knew that creating this business wasn't achievable on my own, so I took other steps to help me get to where I needed to be: I hired a business coach.

- **Relevant.** To have a relevant plan, it needs to align with the big-picture vision that you have set out for yourself. There's no sense in putting time and energy into something if it's not going to move you toward your purpose.

- **Time-Bound.** The best goals also include information about when the actions should be completed. Additionally, make sure your timing is realistic. The bigger the change, the longer you should expect it to take.

To make time-bound goals, you can choose specific time frames. You might say you want to accomplish your goal within the next week, month, or year. You can also break up bigger goals into smaller steps. If you know you want to accomplish something within the next year, ensure your plan includes weekly actions to keep you on track.

Habits are powerful tools of efficiency. Consider how much time you'd lose each day if you had to concentrate on how to drive, tie your shoes, or brush your teeth. We're able to do these tasks without even thinking about them.

But our habits can also betray us. Focusing on your struggles rather than finding solutions, staying up too late, and creating distractions are all examples of habits that fail to support peace and happiness. However, by adding a few good habits and eliminating a few bad ones, you'll soon be well on your way to making drastic changes in your life.

Questions for Reflection

What are your less I do (LID) excuses?

What things do you believe or tell yourself that keep you from exploring your full potential? What internal factors keep you from moving forward with your plan?

_____

_____

_____

_____

How can you implement behavior changes in your life?

Pick just one thing you'd like to adjust and walk through the five stages of behavior change. What might each stage look like?

_____

_____

_____

_____

What habit do you want to change?

Think through the previous steps of the SHAPE framework—story, hone, and assess. Based on what you know about yourself and your goals, what is just one habit that could move you closer to your vision?

_____

_____

_____

_____

How would you go about changing this habit?

Write down a specific action plan. Does this require replacing a bad habit with something better? Does it involve adopting an all-new behavior? How could you form this habit in a way that sets you up for success?

_____

_____

_____

_____

How can you avoid pitfalls when starting your new habit?

What are some difficulties you predict you'll face? How can you lessen or prevent these challenges?

_____

_____

_____

_____

Activity: Create a Plan for Success

While keeping your vision at the forefront of your mind, design an action plan. Think about your purpose and what you need to get there. Look back to the work you did during the assess step. What tools, skills, or experiences did you determine that you needed? Craft a plan that will help you access those things. Look for resources within your community or reach out to a mentor. Decide when you want to accomplish your goals and mark it in your calendar. Make sure that all of your goals are SMART.

STEP 5: Execution

What are you doing right now to work towards your vision?

CHAPTER 9:

Quality of Life Theory

"Self-care is not selfish. You cannot serve
from an empty vessel."

—Eleanor Brown

Many academic fields, including psychology, international development, economics, and healthcare, talk about quality of life. There isn't a single definition of this term, but it generally refers to how a person feels about multiple different aspects of their life.

The World Health Organization (WHO) describes quality of life as "an individual's view of their position in life in relation to their objectives, aspirations, standards, and worries and in the context of the culture and value systems in which they live." Quality of life is a personal indicator of well-being.

Quality of life has also become an important concept in medicine. In the past, doctors primarily focused on helping people live as many years as possible. In the later 20th century, many care providers began to recognize the importance of ensuring these years were enjoyable. Now, more health professionals are focused on meeting a person's needs related to their overall well-being.

Elements That Affect Quality of Life

One way to think about your quality of life is to consider the degree to which you are able to lead the life you desire. Your quality of life is typically related to many different connected elements. Some of the elements that may influence your quality of life include your:

- Diet
- Physical activity levels
- Overall health, including your physical, mental, emotional, or spiritual health
- Relationships
- Education
- Income and wealth
- Work environment
- Participation in community or feelings of social belonging
- Sense of dignity, self-respect, safety, or freedom

Without some of these elements, you may have fewer options when it comes to deciding how you want to conduct your life. You can't always directly control all of these elements. Some, such as your education level or health levels, can be improved, although it may take a significant amount of time.

Many of these elements are also interconnected. For example, building stronger feelings of self-respect or self-confidence may give you the courage to explore additional educational opportunities, which could eventually lead to increased income.

Quality of life is often thought about differently across different fields of study. Psychologists tend to place less emphasis on elements like food and money, for example. Instead, they focus more on intangible mental experiences like pleasant feelings, life satisfaction, and overall well-being.

You can decide what quality of life means for you. If you close your eyes and imagine living your best life, what do you see? What's your environment like? What are you doing? Who are the people that surround you? How do you feel?

As you work through the SHAPE framework, the ultimate goal is getting to a better quality of life. This process can help you better understand your current needs, define the quality of life elements that are most important to your ideal vision of what you want your life to look like, and form a plan for achieving improved well-being. A good quality of life is the ultimate outcome of moving through SHAPE.

Enhance Your Quality of Life

The path you take to reach a better quality of life is highly individual. As you ask yourself what a good quality of life means for you, your next steps will become more clear. It will start to become obvious which habits you need to get rid of and which behaviors you need to adopt to get to where you want to be.

Improving your quality of life is a never-ending process. You won't wake up one day with a perfect life that doesn't require any additional changes. Instead, you'll make small adjustments to your daily habits, slowly and gradually leading to bigger changes. Once you accomplish certain goals, you'll likely set new ones. Achieving a good quality of life is an ongoing process, not a single destination.

Concentrate on the areas of your life that you can influence. There are plenty! Try to let go of the things you don't have control over. Remember to monitor your progress by periodically reflecting in a journal or taking a quality-of-life evaluation. You may be more inspired to keep going if you can see your progress.

CHAPTER 10

Execution

"Between stimulus and response there is a space. In that space is our power to choose our response. In our response lies our growth and freedom."

—Viktor Frankl

It's easy to reflect, organize, and prepare, but putting those plans into action can be hard. However, if you spend all of your time dreaming and never make time for *doing*, you'll never get anywhere!

The last crucial step of the SHAPE method involves making your SMART plan happen in real life. The execution step will allow you to regularly participate in stress management practices that provide transformation, clarity, and optimal health and wellness. In this final stage, you will put your plan in motion so that you can be your best, do your best, and give your best.

"Execution" is defined as the carrying out or putting into effect a plan, order, or course of action. *Carrying and putting* are the keywords here, as they are action words that indicate momentum.

In December 2020, I was sitting in my home office wearing a heather gray Martha's Vineyard sweatshirt, black leggings, and had a blanket draped over my lap while looking at the screen with my oversized eyeglasses. I was on a virtual mentorship call developing a 2021 business vision. I wanted to create a space to empower nurses and healthcare providers to manage stress to optimize their personal and professional development, health, and overall well-being more effectively. It was a vision I had curated in my mind, but I hadn't yet seen it through. Sometimes, I thought it would never truly happen. However, despite the self-doubt, I dutifully scratched out a plan in tightly written cursive.

Often, we mentally block or shut down our brilliant ideas with self-doubt or limiting beliefs, which can impact our effort—or lack thereof. Our idea becomes stuck in the space between our ears, and we rob the world of our brilliance. Think about a time when you allowed fear, uncertainty, or feelings of discomfort to keep your thoughts trapped in your head, like a baby in the mother's womb. Don't spend too much time walking around pregnant. Birth your ideas out into the world!

Many of us start the new year with a vision board, new year resolution, or word of intention. Sometimes, we even often set forth the steps to execute this phenomenon. However, we rarely take the time to develop a contingency plan for sustainability.

Leaning on Others
To Keep Your Plan Alive

One thing I have learned is that you can't reach your full potential while going it alone. Surrounding yourself with a network of mentors, peers, and mentees keeps you sharp, enables lifelong learning, and provides you with resources when times get tough.

A way to birth your brilliance is to cultivate community, accountability, support, and education (CASE):

- **Community** is formed when you surround yourself with like-minded people who understand and respect your vision. Ideally, these people are also actively pursuing and executing their own visions. Together, you can help each other grow.

If you're lucky, you already have a community around you. You may have co-workers, friends, or peers walking a similar path. To build your community, look for associations or organizations in your field and get involved. Use social media to connect with people who are doing work that resonates with you. Meet up with peers to network and bounce ideas off of each other.

- **Accountability** is born when you find someone who will hold your feet to the fire so you stay en route to your destination. This person is aware of your vision and execution plan and will give you honest feedback. They can help you stay on track, offer advice, and allow you to gain clarity when things seem a bit cloudy.

Your accountability partner may be a coach or mentor who can relate to you through their past experiences. Alternatively, you can serve in co-accountability roles with a peer and help each other stay on track. You may even be able to form a small accountability group with others in your community.

Routinely schedule meetings with your accountability partner or group. You can meet once a month or even once a week depending on your needs. During these meetings, try reviewing your plan and setting new goals. When you next meet with your accountability partner, report your progress. You may find that you are more likely to follow through when someone else is paying attention to how you're proceeding.

- **Support** can provide the fuel you need to keep going. While you can definitely find support in your community, it is also important to cultivate external support from family and friends. These individuals may not always understand exactly what you're doing, but they'll be sitting in the front row during your successes with open arms, ready to embrace you and say good job. They'll also be there to help pick you up when you stumble.

You can build a support network by talking about your goals and sharing success stories with your loved ones. It may also help to cultivate additional supportive friendships by striking up conversations at work, school, church, or any other places you regularly spend time. To meet new people, join a new group, or start a hobby.

Having a support network of people unfamiliar with your work can significantly combat your stress levels. While it's good to be driven, it's also important to regularly let your mind rest, and having enjoyable non-work-related conversations with people you care about is a great way to accomplish that. And remember that support goes both ways. Make sure to regularly ask your loved ones about their own goals and accomplishments!

- **Education** is the knowledge you receive from an expert with the background and experience to provide the road map to your destination. This doesn't necessarily mean you have to go back to school or take a formal class. It can also include connecting with a mentor in your current or desired field. These individuals can connect you with other people who have the ability to make your dreams happen, introduce you to new resources, and offer solutions based on their own more extensive experience.

To find a mentor, look for someone who has gone through experiences that match your goals and has already achieved the type of success you are aiming for. This person should also be enthusiastic about sharing their knowledge and willing to offer feedback.

You may be able to find a mentor by reaching out to people you already know. Perhaps a current or past boss is willing to take you under their wing! You may also meet potential mentors through networking and meeting more people in your field. A surefire way to work with a mentor with the ability and expertise to help is by hiring a coach. These individuals thoroughly understand their field and have the expertise and willingness to teach others.

Focusing on CASE and surrounding yourself with people who understand you, keep you accountable, cheer you on, and teach you new things will help you execute your plan and keep your vision alive in the long term. Going it alone is a surefire way to increase your stress levels, so building CASE into your daily routine can invite more peace into your life.

Executing a Vision

In 2021, I launched my company, The Stress Blueprint, to carry out my forecasted vision from 2020. The word launch sounds fancy, but all I did was put my plan into action. I began by recruiting a few oncology nurses to join the six-week pilot Nurse Wellness Mentorship (NWM) that I had outlined on my vision cast template.

I was totally stressed out because I was out of my comfort zone. As my mentor, Dr. Avis Jones Deweever, would say, "People have to pay to access your brilliance." Up to this point, I was a healthcare professional who had spent over $250,000 for higher education as well as personal and professional development, and I was used to serving without expecting to be compensated. This was new territory for me.

I often felt like I was building a plane while flying it, but the most important point is that I was in the air and taking action. The main driving force behind my journey was the community, accountability, support, and education (CASE) I received through Dr. Avis' mentorship program. A vision is foundational for takeoff, but CASE is essential for sustainability while you're flying.

The NWM changed the lives of the nurses who were enrolled. As a result of the program, my nurses significantly reduced their stress levels, improved their work/life balance, strengthened their personal relationships, increased their confidence, and enhanced their self-care abilities. As a nurse with a scientific background, I collected objective and subjective data to validate my idea and provide proof of concept.

The NWM program included pre-recorded modules with worksheets, weekly motivational recordings, weekly live mentoring, and a virtual supportive community. The beta participants included four nurses—three Registered Nurses and one Licensed Practical Nurse

The program used the Perceived Stress Scale, a tool commonly used in clinical research about stress, to assess stress levels before and after the program. After the nurses completed the program, 75% of the participants experienced reductions in stress levels. For one person, stress levels were lowered by 66%!

Based on these pilot results, I redeveloped the NWM as a twelve-week program. Every participant who enrolled in the second cohort of the program had moderate levels of stress, but after the program's completion, all of the nurses had lower stress levels. The participants' stress levels were reduced by 35-63%! Although building this program and introducing it to the world was one of the scariest things I've ever done, I can clearly see that my work—my vision of what I'm trying to achieve through helping others— is paying off.

The Nurse Wellness Mentorship was an amazing experience that laid the foundation for my later work with The Stress Blueprint. In this company, I empower individuals and organizational teams to transform their personal and professional lives through stress management by leveraging emotions. I love to work with individuals who are ready to transform their lives and shift their mindset to see challenges as growth opportunities, gain clarity on and align with their purpose, develop strategies to improve their relationships, and learn how to create, identify, and celebrate golden moments in their life.

My assessments and client feedback have shown that the tools I have designed, including the SHAPE framework, are transformative. My clients have left my training and coaching sessions feeling more empowered to navigate change and conflict, adopt growth mindsets, develop more flexibility and agility, and use individualized tools to manage stress.

We underestimate the power of our abilities to change lives. We all, including YOU, have the potential and right to take up space in this world and make a difference. We have gifts to share with the world, and to access and execute those gifts, stress management is pivotal. Imagine if I allowed my internal stressors—limiting beliefs and self-doubt—to prevent me from starting The Stress Blueprint program. The people who I served would not be their BEST, do their BEST, and give their BEST in this world.

Participant Testimonials for The Stress Blueprint

"Prior to participating in this program, I was unaware how much stress has impacted my life and my health. Wendy's program has brought about self-awareness of my internal and external stressors and has taught me effective ways in dealing with my stress."
—*Jenny*

"Before the program, I had a lot of stress and was overwhelmed with competing priorities in my life. I found it hard to shut my mind off many times, especially at night. As I went through the program, I was able to reframe the challenging aspects of my life as opportu-

nities for growth. Now, I am able to sleep better, and I prioritize things in my life much better. I've really honed in on my professional and personal goals, and this program was integral in that change."
—Elaine

"Since being in this program, I stopped seeing my therapist and feel like I have a handle on my stress."
—Ashley

"Throughout our lives, we take classes, are provided tools, and are encouraged to 'do it,' but we often don't know how to employ these tools. The support, direction, tools, and tasks provided, coupled with encouragement and belief in me, have guided me to better manage the stress in my life. It forced me to set goals for myself. It helped me identify negative and positive triggers in my life. It brought Ho'oponopono [a Hawaiian practice related to forgiveness and setting things right] into my life. I looked into the depth of my inner self. It taught me to be mindful of my inner self and how I control my energy and the power of our inner thoughts. Affirmations are important. It taught me to feed myself socially, emotionally, physically, environmentally, intellectually, spiritually, financially and occupationally. I learned that I am independent but fragile, fulfilled but empty. I am a whole and a part of a whole. I am confident in myself. I have added value. I am not afraid of retiring anymore. I know I will be okay. I have set boundaries, physically and emotionally, so I can be my best self and keep my goals in front of me and obtainable."
—Sharon

Insert Your Story Here

Now, let's talk about you. What vision are you harboring? Which stressors are preventing you from aligning with your purpose? What are you willing to do to release your vision into the world? Who makes up your CASE that can help drive your vision forward?

By carefully following the tools and exercises laid out in this book, you can be well on your way to SHAPE-ing your best life. If, along the way, you need a coach or mentor, require accountability, or want to be connected to a community, let me know how I can help by visiting www.stressblueprint.com!

Questions for Reflection

What are your next steps?

In the Plan step of the SHAPE framework, you outlined some goals. Now, it's time to decide what to tackle first. What small steps can you take right now that will bring you closer to your purpose?

_____

_____

_____

_____

How can you make your plan sustainable?

Identify some resources you can turn to when you're stressed to keep your momentum going.

Community: Which groups of like-minded individuals can you join together with?

_____

_____

_____

_____

Accountability: Who can help hold your feet to the fire and give honest feedback?

_____

_____

_____

_____

Support: Which loved ones can you rely on to stand by your side?

_____

_____

_____

Education: Where can you find a coach or mentor to provide expert advice?

_____

_____

_____

_____

Activity:
Put Your Plan in Motion

No more writing or reflecting. Now, it's time to take action! Put down this book and take a step toward living the life you've been dreaming of. As you work, think about how best to develop your network and add CASE to your plan.

Made in the USA
Columbia, SC
14 September 2024

42138002R00089